Tracking Significant Achievement in the *Early Years*

Second Edition

Child-centred assessment in the Foundation Stage

Vicky Hutchin

Hodder & Stoughton

A MEMBER OF THE HODDER HEADLINE GROUP

This book was first published in the *Tracking Significant Achievement* series, edited by Shirley Clarke and Barry Silsby.

Acknowledgements
The author wishes to thank Vicky Hurst, Gill Collins and Janet Rose for their comments, and Margaret Lally for suggesting she write this book. Most importantly, she wishes to thank Tess Robson and the staff and parents of Tachbrook Nursery School, and Janine Davenall at Churchill Gardens Primary School.

Since the first edition of this book, Vicky Hurst has, sadly, died. She will be greatly missed by many in the early childhood education field.

Order queries: please contact Bookpoint Ltd, 130 Milton Park, Abingdon, Oxon OX14 4SB.
Telephone: (44) 01235 827720, Fax: (44) 01235 400454. Lines are open from 9.00–6.00, Monday to Saturday, with a 24 hour message answering service.
Email address: order@bookpoint.co.uk

British Library Cataloguing in Publication Data
A catalogue record for this title is available from The British Library

ISBN 0 340 79083 0
First published 1996
Second edition 2000

Impression number   9   8   7   6   5   4   3   2
Year   2005   2004   2003   2002   2001

Copyright © 1996, 2000 Vicky Hutchin

Printed in Great Britain for Hodder & Stoughton Educational, the educational publishing division of Hodder Headline Plc, 338 Euston Road, London NW1 3BH, by J W Arrowsmith, Bristol.

Contents

This book is written primarily for teachers in nursery schools and classes and in reception classes, but is equally appropriate for those working in the many other settings for 3, 4 and 5 year olds where staff other than teachers – particularly nursery nurses and nursery officers in schools and daycare centres – are involved in the assessment and record-keeping process. Where the text at times uses the term 'teacher', this should be taken to refer to all of the trained staff involved.

Tracking Significant Achievement in the Early Years

The purpose of this book

Over the past few years, developing a useful, comprehensive yet practical system for teacher assessment has proved problematic. Several local education authorities (LEAs) recommended that it should be based on regular, detailed observations of children in every aspect of learning. For many teachers this became unwieldy and too time-consuming. Other LEAs developed systems of assessment based on checklists of skills, but these could only give a limited and generalised view of any child.

More recently, the focus for primary teachers' assessments of children's learning has been to look for **significant achievement.** We believe this is also the best way forward for the ongoing assessment of children in nursery and reception classes.

This book aims to establish a coherent and manageable framework for organising ongoing assessment in the classroom, in which significant achievement is the focus. The underpinning principles for this are:

◆ the assessment process must include the child, aiming for the child to become part of the evaluation process;
◆ the assessment process must enhance the child's learning and the teacher's teaching;
◆ all assessment processes should be manageable.

This chapter describes good assessment practice, from the planning stage to assessment and record-keeping. It deals with the issue of defining significant achievement and how to look for it and recognise it.

Chapter 2 looks at good assessment practice within the context of the early years, so it considers good practice, organisation and resource provision which will enable significant achievement to take place and to be recognised.

Chapter 3 provides a variety of examples of significant achievement, derived from teachers' work in early years classrooms, covering different aspects of significant achievement in nursery and reception classes across the curriculum appropriate to this age range.

Chapter 4 sets out typical stages of significant achievement in the early years. The purpose of this is to provide guidance to assist teachers in deciding what might be important and significant in a child's development in different areas of the curriculum.

Chapter 5 has a question-and-answer format, covering all the issues that arose in the courses and trialling carried out with teachers. It is followed by a final chapter on 'Getting Started'.

Defining assessment and its purpose

Mary Jane Drummond (1993) has a definition of assessment which clearly describes the process as it takes place in the classroom. She sets it out as three crucial questions which educators must ask themselves when they consider children's learning. Those questions are:

◆ *What is there to see?*
◆ *How best can we understand what we see?*
◆ *How can we put our understanding to good use?*

'*What is there to see?*' refers to the fact that we need to be able to access children's understanding in the best possible way. We need to be constantly talking to children about their work, and maximising the opportunities for them to achieve in the first place and demonstrate their achievement in the second. In order to see, the teacher must allow herself time to observe the children, not just in the more structured classroom activities and situations, but in the play situations provided as well. It is often here that children may be operating at their highest levels, clearly demonstrating their achievements.

'How best can we understand what we see?' is the next stage. We need to be able to create a climate in the classroom where teachers are not simply hypothesising about the reasons for children's understanding, but have as much information as possible about this coming from the children themselves. We also need to be clear about our own learning intentions for children, and the learning possibilities within activities and areas of provision, so that we know what is potentially achievable and what we would like children to be able to learn. Flexibility is essential, because what a child does and achieves might not be directly in line with what we expected, but might be just as important and significant for that child.

We need to remember that children learn from *all* their experiences of life, of which school learning is only a part.

'How can we put our understanding to good use?' is the key factor in moving children forwards. If the teacher has answered the first two questions, then the information gathered should give clear indications as to what should be the next move in helping a child to continue to progress.

The purpose of the assessment process is to make explicit children's achievements, celebrate their achievements with them, then help them to move forward to the next goal. Without children's involvement in the assessment process, assessment becomes a judgmental activity, resulting in a one-way view of a child's achievement. Observing the children is an important tool for all staff, but it is always important, wherever possible, to share this with the child, in order to ensure that your interpretation does not become judgmental. When shared with the child, assessment information is more likely to result in a raising of standards, because the child is more focused, motivated and aware of her or his own capabilities and potential. Good assessment practice enables children to be able to fulfil their learning potential and raises self-esteem and self-confidence.

'Assessment' can sometimes be used as the term for what is, in fact, record-keeping. Assessment is understanding children's understanding, record-keeping is recording it, and we are suggesting in this book that it is children's *significant achievement* which needs to be recorded. This should be recorded as a form of Record of Achievement which consists of examples of a child's achievement, commented on in a positive way and stating clearly what the actual achievement was.

It is neither a statutory requirement nor useful to keep samples of children's work at set points in time simply as proof of attainment, whereas Records of Achievement are a motivating and useful aspect of the assessment process.

The planning, assessment and record-keeping cycle: a practical solution

The pre-planning stage

If assessment is to be worthwhile, it is clear that we must first maximise the opportunities for children's achievement, by giving them the best possible learning experiences. A number of support structures within the school and good planning will assist in this.

In some form or other, all experiences and areas of provision in early years classrooms, just as for other age groups, need to be planned and evaluated. This includes areas of provision which are considered to be permanent fixtures (sand, water, role play area, for example), in order to make sure that the provision and its resourcing allows children to develop the skills, knowledge and understanding that the staff would wish, and that it allows for progression, as well as breadth, of learning.

There have been many changes over the past few years to the way the early years curriculum is viewed by the DFEE and OFSTED. Nursery and reception have now become the Foundation Stage, and the curriculum for this stage covers children of 3, 4 and 5 years. The Foundation Stage incorporates a curriculum for *all* young children – in playgroups, day care settings and private nurseries, as well as state schools.

The curriculum is seen as covering six areas of learning: personal, social and emotional development; communication, language and literacy; mathematical development; knowledge and understanding of the world; physical development and creative development. However, it is important to remember that in the early years it is not appropriate to see teaching in terms of narrow subject focus. Children do not learn under subject headings, although it is important that staff use these to plan, to ensure that there is full breadth of curriculum coverage. What is essential is that teachers are aware of the learning possibilities of the activities and areas of provision offered to the children.

Well managed, good quality topic boxes are an excellent idea and should be of use however you choose to plan. These might be for a particular theme used to develop an area of the classroom – for example, a particular kind of shop, a hairdressers, cafe, etc – as well as for the kind of cross-curricular topics used to plan a topic for any age across the primary school. They will need to be reviewed and evaluated from time to time, to check that they are appropriate for the particular occasion and age group and that the resources are of good quality and up to date.

The planning stage

The single most important feature of good planning is to have well thought out learning intentions before any creation of activities and areas of provision. Traditionally in schools and nursery provision, planning entailed devising a simple notion of learning aims for each area of learning, followed by a detailed brainstorm of activities linked to a topic, often in the form of a topic web. Very often, it is the creation of so many activities which causes manageability problems for teachers, thereby reducing flexibility or resulting in the planned curriculum being quite different from what is actually going on. It can also lead to a ticklist approach, where getting through the activities is more important than responding to the way children react to them. It is children's learning which must be our main concern, *not* our plans or schemes of work. They should support the learning, not hinder it.

There is sometimes a concern voiced amongst early years teachers that careful planning will result in a loss of autonomy for the children, too much teacher-directed activity, and a loss of flexibility and spontaneity. However, this is not the case unless all that is planned are narrowly focused teacher-directed activities, with the rest of the provision just happening to exist. Careful planning which looks at all the provision in terms of its learning content is more likely to ensure that children can have meaningful experiences, have access to adult time and the full curriculum. It needs to (*a*) include areas permanently provided (such as the home corner, sand, water, construction area) which children can choose to use independently, (*b*) ensure that the right kind of resources are accessible to children, and (*c*) allow for spontaneity and autonomy and encourage self-motivation. It also needs to include the planning of adult time so that the time spent with groups or individuals is maximised.

Margaret Lally (1991) gives a useful and full account of many of the issues relating to early years planning relevant to both nursery and reception teachers.

The planning stage needs to incorporate both medium-term and short-term planning – for example, termly/half-termly, as well as weekly/daily planning. As Margaret Lally says, it is careful planning that makes spontaneous learning possible. We know the kinds of events – such as the finding of minibeasts, a fall of snow, a local building site – which are likely to generate immediate interest from the children, but unless we are prepared in advance with support structures, such as topic boxes, we will not be able to follow up these interests.

Medium-term planning

We have approached the medium-term planning process by focusing on the following aspects: *planning for curriculum areas and areas of provision, planning for areas of learning* and *planning a topic or theme*.

Planning for curriculum areas and areas of provision

Over recent years early years teachers have increasingly moved towards providing more of a 'workshop' approach in their planning, dividing the classroom into areas which lend themselves to a particular curricular focus, where children can help themselves to a range of available resources.

A creative workshop area might have a range of resources for children to make 2D and 3D objects, to draw, paint and explore a variety of materials. When thoughtfully resourced, this can be ideal in allowing for real differentiation, and for the teacher to be involved at the appropriate level for each child. Similarly, a writing workshop area would provide a range of useful resources, including made-up blank books of various kinds as well as paper, envelopes and various writing aids (alphabet, useful words, examples of writing, names). A science area may have a specific topic focus around a display, with a range of resources for the children's explorations.

Termly or half-termly planning of these areas means examining the potential curriculum coverage of these areas (language and literacy, knowledge and understanding of the world, etc), the corresponding learning intentions, the necessary resources to make this possible, and the possible roles that staff are likely to take on to ensure that learning takes place.

Planning for areas of learning

Planning directly from the areas of learning of the Early Learning Goals in the medium-term would mean taking an area of learning, such as mathematical development, and deciding what you want the children to learn and the kind of learning experiences they need to have. The mathematical potential of each area in the classroom (e.g. in the block area, the water play area, etc) would then be examined in the light of these needs. Some specific activities would also need to be planned to ensure that all the learning intentions are met.

Planning a topic or theme

A theme or topic is often used as a focus for planning over a half term, in early years classrooms as for other age groups. In the early years these might arise out of a particular event, or an interest expressed by the children, which can then be looked at in terms of learning intentions within the various areas of the curriculum. The purpose of a topic or theme is to create a *context* for the children's learning and for the teacher's planning. The areas of learning are often used as the headings under which learning intentions and related specific activities and events might be placed. However, it is important to remember that other things also need to go on simultaneously which might not easily be incorporated into a topic. For younger children, who might find it difficult to focus on other children's or adult's choice of topic, it is important to make sure that the classroom provides a breadth of planned provision outside the topic.

Brainstorming a particular topic with the children is a very useful starting point. This is rarely done with very young children, but can be just as fruitful as with older children. It will provide vital planning information, possible directions and starting points, and interests to follow, as well as revealing the aspects of the topic that the children do not know about or think of. It will also give the teacher clues to the differentiation range. For younger children this might best be done in smaller groups, giving plenty of listening time to the children's ideas and thoughts.

Short-term planning

It is the short-term plans which ensure that the provision and the activities are appropriate to the children for whom they are intended. They will need to be adjusted from day to day so that specific issues can be followed up. It is this planning which needs to incorporate the individual observations and assessments made, as well as the broader learning intentions for groups of children.

Learning intentions need to be seen not just in terms of teacher-initiated and -directed activities, but also to be incorporated into child-initiated activities. For example, as a child is playing in the home corner dressing dolls, a specific learning intention could be incorporated into the play, in order to extend mathematical skills and learning by asking the child: *'Could you sort out all the dolls clothes that you think might fit the largest dolls?'*

Short-term plans can be seen as operating in three ways: *plans for individual children, plans for small groups* and *plans for spontaneous adult involvement.*

Plans for individual children

This kind of planning results from a noted significant achievement or possibly a need to look for it with a particular child – in other words, an observation made or a need to observe. The teacher must be very clear about what is appropriate for the child to move onto next, whether this is to do with social development or a particular skill or concept. For example, a child who is at the stage of being really interested in covering paper with glue, and keeps on adding more glue to the paper, is more concerned with transporting the glue from pot to paper and covering the paper, than with making a particular geometric pattern with cut-out shapes. It is unlikely in this context to be useful to the child to ask her/him to make a particular pattern, but it might be appropriate to talk about the qualities of the glue, to get her/him to look at the changes as it dries and at different ways of covering things (e.g. painting in different ways, sand play, etc).

For another child who has already shown interest in fitting shapes together in block play, making geometric patterns out of shapes could be a very appropriate way of enhancing understanding and knowledge about shape, and increasingly complex challenges could be set: *'Make a spiky pattern', 'See if you can cover the paper in triangles without leaving any spaces', 'Could you do this with circles?'*

Both of these children could be supported in their learning at the same time, especially if the teacher is aware of the child's own stage of development and the possibility for learning in such provision.

Plans for small groups

These can be for a specific group of children or several groups, and are most likely to be teacher-initiated and -directed. The teacher needs to explain her specific intentions to children. These might not be rigidly adhered to, but explaining the learning intentions means that children understand the purpose in the teacher's mind.

Plans for spontaneous adult involvement

This means deciding what area of provision you need to

spend time in, or which children to spend time with, regardless of where they are. Allowing children to be as independent as possible will help allow for the maximum amount of adult involvement without interruptions. Such involvement will include and arise from the staff making observations on an area or on specific children.

Short-term plans might need to be flexible, but nevertheless the teacher needs to be clear about the learning intentions she has for individuals and groups within the class. As Margaret Lally states, *'In the absence of clear intentions and expectations, provision can become static and standards can slip.'* It is by talking to and observing the child in different areas of provision that we decide what the next appropriate learning intentions need to be.

Making assessments in the classroom

Setting up the assessment dialogue

Once you are sure of the learning possibilities in the areas of provision and your own intentions when setting up specific activities, the next step is to let children into the secret!

This can be done in different ways depending on the situation. For example, it could be when introducing children to a new area of provision, or introducing new children to an area, letting them know the kinds of things which would be expected or could be done. It could also take place by getting the children to help plan and set up some new provision, explaining to them, in an appropriate way, what they would be learning about as a result of their own suggestions along with yours.

As already described, some activities will be teacher-initiated and some will be child-initiated, but both will have learning intentions. If it is a teacher-initiated activity, say *why* you want them to do the activity. This can be explained to the group, pairs or individuals. It will let them know what you are expecting from them, and significant achievement can be looked for within this context.

It is important that children are let into the secret for two reasons:

◆ First, because knowing the purpose focuses the child towards a particular outcome. Very often, children have no idea why they have been asked to do something, and they can only look for clues or 'guess what's in the teacher's mind' as a means of knowing what is expected of them.

◆ It will help children not only to become more reflective and aware of what they may be learning, but also to evaluate what they are doing for themselves.

However, many of the situations in which significant achievement is noted will not be specific 'assessment situations' resulting from set tasks and challenges. Spotting significant achievement relies on the teacher being able to observe the children as they are busy in a variety of activities and play situations. The teacher can then ask the child about it afterwards. For example: *'I saw you playing outside today. You were building something and then you set the table. You made sure each person had a knife and fork. Your play looked very interesting. Can you tell me about it?'* Some follow-up questions could relate to more specific learning you spotted, for example about shape, or one-to-one correspondence, or a social skill.

The advantage for the teacher in asking the children how they are doing in relation to the 'shared secret' or learning criteria is that it is a powerful strategy for accessing information about children's progress. This type of questioning invites the child to play an active part in her or his learning. Children who are used to being asked such questions readily respond, because they are beginning to understand that the purpose of the teacher's questions is to help their learning process. The answers children give often put a teacher fully in the picture about the child's level of understanding, as well as why something now appears to have happened (e.g. *'Lisa helped me'*, *'I didn't want to play with Sam because I wanted to do it like this'*, etc).

What we have described in this section constitutes the assessment process at its best. It describes the means by which the teacher makes all her ongoing decisions about children's learning and what they need to do next. Most of the insights gleaned from this continuous dialogue simply inform day-to-day decisions and it is unnecessary to record them. However, when significant achievement occurs, there is a need to recognise and record the event.

Looking for significant achievement and recording it

Record-keeping must have a purpose. If a teacher is to spend time writing things down, it must be useful to both teacher and child. If record-keeping is focused on children's significant achievement, it fulfils many purposes. First, however, we need to look closely at what significant achievement is.

Significant achievement is any leap or development in progress; anything which a teacher feels is important enough to write down. It will not happen very often, or it could not be defined as significant. It might be the first time a child does something, or it might be when the teacher is sure that a particular skill or concept has now been thoroughly demonstrated (e.g. in a number of contexts, shows an understanding of 'empty' and 'full'). Work with teachers has led us to believe that significant achievement seems to fall into five categories:

◆ **physical skill** (e.g. use of scissors)
◆ **social skill** (e.g. able to take turns)
◆ **attitude development** (e.g. increased confidence)
◆ **conceptual development** (e.g. clear understanding that print conveys meaning)
◆ **process skill** (e.g. able to make a prediction)

These are all examples of possible significant achievement. Clearly, what is significant for one child is not necessarily significant for another. This is a welcome departure from the style of assessment which puts a set of arbitrary criteria, rather than the child's own development, as the basis of one's judgements. Although the first two categories are covered by curriculum areas in the early years (physical development and personal, social and emotional development), an achievement in *any* area of learning may be physical or social.

The more examples of significant achievement one sees, the clearer the idea becomes. If a child is a relatively slow learner, it does not mean that the child will have no significant achievement. It simply means that significance has to be redefined for that child. For instance, in learning to say goodbye to his mother, a child who finds this difficult might make several steps of significant achievement (e.g. allowing her to leave for ten minutes, etc, until able to accept this for a whole session), whereas another child might start nursery being able to do this without distress.

Talking to children about their significant achievements

The *context* within which significant achievement can be spotted is usually the ongoing assessment dialogue, although it might be demonstrated by a product, such as a piece of writing the child has done. When significant achievements occur, they can be underplayed in a busy classroom. Children have the right to have *all* their significant achievements recognised, understood and recorded. Recognition consists of simply informing the child (e.g. *'Well done, that is the first time you have tidied up after yourself'*).

Understanding *why* the significant event took place is a crucial part of this process. It consists of asking the child why the significance occurred. In trialling with teachers, we found that the child's answer often contradicts what the teacher saw as the reason for the significant achievement. This is an important discovery, because it shows that we must find out, from the child, *why* the significant achievement occurs if we are to be able to follow up the achievement with appropriate teaching strategies. One example of a piece of work brought to a course on significant achievement demonstrates the importance of finding out why the achievement took place. The child is not in an early years class, but this is irrelevant in this context. The point here is the importance of asking the child why something significant took place:

❛ *Ben chose for the first time to be a scribe in shared writing. Shared writing had been going on for over a year, with children in pairs, and this was significant for*

Ben. The teacher believed that the reason this had happened was because of the context of the story ('Horrible Red Riding Hood'-from the wolf's point of view), and her decision was to do more 'reverse' fairy stories as a way of encouraging Ben. However, when asked on the course to go back and ask Ben why he had done this, the teacher reported that Ben said 'It was because you put me with Matthew, and he's shy, like me.' *The implications for the teacher now are considerably different. Clearly Ben is sensitive to the dominance of the child he is working with, and the teacher's way forward now is to consider his pairing more carefully, both for writing and perhaps for other curriculum areas.* **❞**

At first the children might find it difficult to answer why the significant achievement has occurred, as this may well be an unfamiliar form of questioning. However, opening up the dialogue with children is an important step and shows that you value their views. At first it may need to be quite factual: *'You seemed to be enjoying ... today. Tell me what you were doing.'* Or: *'You managed to write your name all by yourself today, can you tell me what helped you?'*

The child should be central to the recognition and recording of the comment. When the achievement occurs, the teacher, in a one-to-one situation, needs to make much of the event.

For bilingual children who are at the beginning stages in learning English, it will be helpful to demonstrate what you are talking about with visual clues, e.g. taking the child to the area in which the significant achievement occurred, or pointing to what you think was significant in a piece of work.

Do not expect answers from all the children to come straight away, but continue with introducing the dialogue on every possible occasion. It will certainly give them the idea that you feel what they have been doing is an achievement, and begin to get them to become more reflective themselves.

The Record of Achievement

Many local authorities have developed something similar to a Record of Achievement (which would be used for older children) specifically for the early years. Sometimes these are in the form of a diary of observations or a profile. The Record of Achievement we are suggesting here would contain all the samples of significant achievement for each child. It is important that they are shared with, and preferably compiled with, the child, and in this way can have a highly motivating effect.

Sometimes teachers have kept the samples in plastic document wallets to keep them clean, and this way they are easier for younger children to handle and to see their work without it becoming damaged. Several such wallets can then be joined together with string or put in a binder to keep them as a record over time. A record like this would be likely to contain photos of 3D work (such as a model), drawings and writing (which could be photocopies) and non-product-style significant achievement (e.g. the example of the child settling in) and observations. All of these will include the notes and comments from the teacher and the child.

An example of a comment for significant achievement might be:

Emma chose today, for the first time, to play with other children. Emma said it was because she wanted to go on the slide.

The formative comment has many benefits:

◆ The child owns the comment and has witnessed it being written, having been asked to say why the significant achievement took place.
◆ Parents and other interested parties find it much more meaningful to focus on the times when a significant formative comment has been written, because they make the progression of the child explicit.
◆ The child and teacher can look back to previous comments at any time, to compare with further progress

and to help know what needs to be targeted for the future.

The summative tracking system

So far, we have described the process of assessment and the accompanying formative record-keeping. However, so that the system is rigorous and children do not fall through the net, there needs to be some kind of summative tracking system. This should not be a burdensome task, so we suggest that a matrix is made with the children's names down the side and the contexts in which significant achievement might occur along the top. These would be, essentially, the teaching contexts. Then, when significant achievement occurs, and the teacher has written the brief formative comment, she keeps track of this by entering the date and a code to show which category of significance occurred:

Child's name	PSE Dev	Physical	Language	Reading	Writing	Maths	K & U	Creative
Pavendeep	settling in 9/99	Climbing ⓐ 2/00		ⓒ name 11/99 ⓐ retelling story 3/00	ⓟ name 12/99 ⓒ dictated story 2/00	ⓒ number 6/00	ICT ⓒ 5/00	ⓟ painting 11/99
Thomas	relating to to adults 12/99	Fine motor ⓟ ⓐ 4/00	ⓢ with peers 2/00		ⓟⓗ list in role play 5/00	ⓒ ⓐ shape + problem solving 3/00	Technol ⓟ 12/99	drawing ⓟ ⓐ 5/00
Chantalle	Settling in 1/00 relating to peers 2/00		ⓐⓟ to group 5/00	ⓟ ⓒ retelling whole book 6/00	ⓟ sign 5/00		ⓟ observing 6/00	
Jerome	settling in 1/00	gross motor 3/00 ⓟ		ⓒ print direction letter recognition 4/00	ⓟⓗ name 5/00	ⓒ time 5/00		

ⓢ = social skill, ⓟⓗ = physical skill, ⓐ = attitude development, ⓟ = process skill, ⓒ = concept

Matrix for tracking significant achievement

This matrix is, of course, only one example of the many ways teachers could track significant achievement. However, the method used should be simple, clear and manageable. The matrix includes a column for social development, to use to track achievements such as settling in to school or nursery, which would not fit under other curriculum areas.

This tracking record can serve a number of functions. At a glance the teacher may see:

◆ a few children who appear to have shown no significant achievement, and therefore need to be focused on, in case they have been missed;
◆ a child who has shown significant achievement in, say, reading, but not in writing, and therefore needs to be observed;
◆ that none of the children has shown any significant achievement in, say, knowledge and understanding of the world, which indicates a need for the teacher to rethink the curriculum on offer;
◆ a bright child who appears to have shown no significant achievement, which indicates that she/he needs to be given more challenging, open-ended tasks.

End-of-year records

Anything passed on to the next teacher needs to be useful to that teacher and able to be read quickly and easily. It is of no use passing on the whole Record of Achievement, because much of the content would have served its purpose and been surpassed by subsequent samples. The best practice, therefore, is to sift the contents down to, for instance, one example each of writing/mark-making, drawing, social development, mathematical development and science. These, together with the record of reading skills and understandings, would be passed on to the next teacher. This will be manageable and useful for the next teacher to read. In the case of children with particular learning difficulties, it might be useful to pass on more samples, perhaps showing the progression across the year. Teachers involved in the trialling of this system felt that it would be unnecessary to pass on the summative tracking matrix, because it is essentially a working document.

Conclusion

This chapter outlines a framework for assessment which puts the child's learning and development first. However, **this approach can also meet the requirements for children from Year 1 onwards.** The following chapters have been carefully constructed to build on this chapter – giving examples of significant achievement and answering the most common questions which teachers ask about looking for significant achievement.

Teachers, in trialling, were inspired and delighted by the fact that, at last, with this system, they could make the focus of their assessment practice the total development of the child, where ***equal status is given to tiny steps*** (*as given in the example of the child progressing towards saying goodbye to his mother*), ***which might otherwise be seen as trivial, and to more traditional demonstrations of progress.*** The feedback has been, overall, that although it takes a while to get used to this different approach, the impact it has on the children's self-esteem and progress, the working atmosphere in the classroom, and children's ability to evaluate and set their own targets is considerable. And, for some children, it has resulted in leaps in progress which teachers have said would not have otherwise occurred.

In their first summer after using tracking significant achievement, teachers said that their end-of-year records had never been easier to write!

2 Learning and Teaching in the Early Years

It is widely acknowledged that the first six years of life represent a period of rapid development. Learning takes place at this time at a faster rate than during any other phase of life. This means that a vast range of physical, social, emotional, intellectual, and linguistic achievements will have taken place for all children *before* they enter nursery at three years of age. For example, for the majority of children, their linguistic development will be such that they will have achieved the ability to communicate effectively through talk in a range of situations, sometimes in more than one language – although they will still have much to learn. They will also have achieved a growing understanding of, and ability to manipulate, the physical and social worlds that surround them, along with a substantial level of control of their own body and movements.

How has all this been possible? It will have taken place without any explicitly formal teaching, mostly through interaction within the family at home. Children are intrinsically motivated to learn from the beginning of babyhood, as they strive to make sense of the world around them. They learn through their play and explorations, following what holds their interest. Most importantly, they learn through building relationships with others, usually beginning in the family. At home, adults support and extend them, sometimes leaving them to play and explore for themselves, at other times remaining highly involved.

Children, just like adults, are different from each other, and recognising these differences is an important part of the teacher's job in assessing what achievement is significant for each child. Nursery and reception teachers are well aware of the differences in levels of development that can exist between children of the same age in their classes. The enormous variations in the experiences children have had in their preschool lives is often a major cause of these differences. The main influence in any child's life is the family, especially in the early years of childhood. Yet each family is very different in many ways. For example, families differ in size – the numbers of adults living in the home and responsible for the children, as well as the numbers of siblings – and in circumstances – whether or not parents are working, the kind of work they do, the kind of living accommodation they have. They also differ in the expectations they have about their children and in what is considered important for children to be doing and to know about.

In addition, there is the variety of different forms of preschool provision that a child entering a reception class may have experienced. For some, reception class may be the first group experience outside the home and immediate family. Others may have attended playgroups, nursery school or class, or a private nursery school or day nursery, since a very young age. Some may have already attended a number of different types of provision. This difference in experience is bound to affect the way a child responds to schooling initially, as well as her/his breadth of knowledge and awareness of the world.

Children also learn at different rates, and some children with similar experience need a great deal more time to explore and to practise than others. Achievements which are significant for one child – for example, being able to cut out a drawing with accuracy and being able to play co-operatively with another child for five minutes – may not be significant for another with a similar experience of the world. On the other hand, explaining how to play a turn-taking game to a small group and then organising the play, or cutting across a piece of paper without adult assistance for the first time, may be a significant achievement for the second child.

For all children entering nursery or reception class, this is the very beginning of their school careers. This means entering an institutional setting where expectations of behaviour and the kind of daily routines that take place will probably differ considerably from anything they have encountered before. Even a child who has already been to nursery for almost two years, on entering reception class will be met with new routines, such as attending assemblies and 'playtimes'. In order to have a smooth transition to school, these expectations and routines need to be made explicit and reasons need to be given for them. Most of all, children will need time to adapt and adjust to them.

Information gathered from parents/carers is essential in enabling the teacher to know from the start what is likely to be significant in each child's development. They know their own child intimately, her/his interests and how she/he has responded to new situations, as well as her/his development. In many ways the 'assessment dialogue' discussed in Chapter 1 should begin in informal discussions with the parent/carer even before the child starts in school or nursery.

How do young children learn?

Young children learn through:

Play

Through play, children explore and investigate, create and imagine, solve problems and practise newly acquired skills. Play is one of the most important means of learning for young children. Piaget emphasised the contribution which play makes to a child's cognitive development. Vygotsky believed that children operate at their highest level during play, especially imaginative play. In play, they are practising skills, using what they already know but also trying out new ideas and skills at their own pace and in their own way. In play, the child is in control and naturally moves between concrete experiences and representing ideas symbolically in a variety of different ways. Being able to move from the concrete experiences to their representation is essential in developing abstract thought.

Social interaction, language and communication

Interaction between adults and children and between the children themselves is an essential means of learning. The quality of interaction between adults and children is very important, as it is adults who are needed to provide the right kind and amount of support to the young child. Vygotsky (1962) called the stage at which learning takes place the *zone of proximal development*. This can be interpreted to mean that what the child needs a degree of help with today, she/he will be able to do alone tomorrow. Infants and children seek out social interaction with others: they are what Bruner (1981) calls *socio-centric* and they need to be active partners in the interaction that takes place. The main means of communication which enables this social interaction to take place is language. Bruner notes how it is the baby's desire to interact with the human beings around which provides much of the motivation to communicate more effectively. This process continues in the development of the young child.

Exploration

Children learn through exploring the environment around them. We all need to be given time to explore when learning something new, whether it is learning a new job, or learning to use a new computer. For children, direct concrete 'hands-on' experiences are essential to learning. They learn through actively doing, and solving problems physically before being able to do this in an abstract way.

Research which has been undertaken throughout the past century has led us to an in-depth and detailed understanding of how young children learn, from birth onwards. This research is of great significance to anyone teaching young children and the following findings from recent research about children's learning need to be taken into account by all those working with young children.

Motivation and active learning Research has shown that, from birth onwards, one of the key factors in learning is the infant's own intrinsic motivation not only to make sense of its surroundings and experiences but to gain some control over these. It is clear that, from the beginning, children are active learners, initiating and seeking to exert some influence on their surroundings.

Language for learning and learning language Language is essential to all learning. Research on the acquisition of language has shown that in the pre-speech stages it is the *baby* who initiates, the mother who replies by talking in response to a movement, a change in gaze or a sound. Gordon Wells' (1986) research has shown how, with young children from the beginning of their speech development, the child as initiator of the communication continues to be important not only in the learning of language but also in all other learning.

Social interaction The overwhelming importance of social interaction in learning is now widely acknowledged. Vygotsky and Bruner both stress the importance of social interaction in learning, as well as the importance of language and communication for the development of thought. As the infant grows older, social interaction with peers also grows in significance. This means that in the school situation the *social context* for learning must be considered as an essential ingredient for success, helping to ensure that meaningful interaction with adults and peers can take place.

Stimulating environment Research has also shown the need for a stimulating and challenging environment for young children if they are to learn successfully. If this is not provided, even babies at a very young age will lose interest and become apathetic. Part of this stimulation must come from responsive adults who engage with the child on what is important to her/him.

Meaningful contexts Donaldson (1978) has shown how learning takes place in contexts which are *meaningful* to the child. Her research on Piaget's work shows the importance of both a social setting and use of language which are familiar to the child in creating a meaningful context for the child. In order to learn effectively, a challenge needs to be offered within a context which is relevant to the child, and which fits with the child's existing understanding and experience.

Learning is not subject-based Children learn in a holistic way. Their learning is not 'compartmentalised' or split up into subjects: this is only done for adult convenience. Children learn the skills, knowledge and understanding they need for a particular situation or task. This will then be generalised to other situations, but it means that social, emotional, physical and cognitive learning is taking place at the same time, in the process of learning to do something or learning about something. This is why the aspects of significant achievement highlighted in Chapter 1 are so important.

As Tina Bruce points out, relationships with others can help or hinder children in their self-motivated learning: *'The difficulty lies in that adults tend to cut across children's self-motivation because of a tendency to be too dominant.'* (1987) This has important implications for all early years staff and the approach they take to teaching. To see children operating at their highest levels, watching them operate in *self-initiated* activities (for example, play) is essential.

Implications for planning and organisation

What we know about how children learn and the necessary conditions to enhance their learning has many implications for staff, not only in planning learning experiences for the children but also in the way these will be organised.

Planning for learning through action and exploration

Planning and organisation must take account of the fact that children learn through physical action and exploration – by trying things out for themselves. They are motivated to explore and to understand the world around them, but need the time and space to do so. Presenting materials in an inviting and imaginative way will encourage children to explore. But teaching in the early years is not *just* a question of giving children the opportunity to explore. It is important that staff are aware of the learning potential in all provision and activities made available. For example, young children can learn a great deal of maths, science and technology through exploring what can be done with wooden blocks, if staff are aware of the potential for learning within this provision. Staff can then guide children's attention to this as they explore and play imaginatively.

Planning for language and social interaction

As social interaction and talk are so important for learning, planning and organisation need to reflect this. Being involved with the children and interacting with them plays an essential part in their learning. This means planning to ensure the maximum time is allowed for the kind of adult-child interaction in which the child is either the initiator or takes on a key role. It will not help the child's understanding when she/he is expected just to agree with the adult, give one-word answers to adults' questions or silently carry out adult directions. When the child initiates the talk, the adult can soon see what is important to the child and the ideas she/he is grappling with. By commenting and making suggestions, the adult can then begin to assist in moving the child's thinking or actions forward. The fact that the adult is responding to the child, rather than the other way around, means that the interaction and the intended learning is set in a context which is relevant to the child – the meaningful context which Donaldson has shown to be so important.

Sometimes it will be important that the staff member initiates the interaction, either to ensure that the child is given a broad range of experiences (in other words, to introduce some new experience to the child) or to find out what the child is thinking or doing. Here it is not only important that we listen to children's responses and give them plenty of time to respond, but that we ask questions in an open-ended way so that their responses are useful to them as well as us. These are some examples of helpful questions:

> *I'd really like to join in your play. Can you tell me what you are doing?'*
> *'Did you enjoy that activity? Tell me about it.'*
> *'How are you getting on ...?'*
> *'What happened when...?'*
> *'Why do you think that happened?*

The important thing is to make sure you give time to listen to all the children in the class, regardless of their ability to express themselves. Shy children and bilingual children at an early stage in learning English may need to be able to communicate at first in other ways, for example through using gesture and visual cues (e.g. taking you to show you what they have done or noticed). However, knowing that some children may take longer to express themselves or may not feel comfortable to talk in a group situation, and planning for this, will soon help them to build up their confidence.

It is also essential that situations are planned so that children can interact meaningfully with each other. We know that the best interaction takes place in pairs, but larger groups can work well for shorter periods. The organisation of the classroom and the outside area should be such as to encourage children to work collaboratively in small groups together.

The implications of extended interaction between both staff and children and children themselves mean that the resources and areas of the classroom and outside need to be arranged so that children can be as independent as possible, able to find the resources they need and to get involved in a wide range of activities without having to interrupt staff.

Planning for a breadth of experiences and a stimulating environment

Children need a rich variety of experiences if we are to ensure that learning takes place for all children across the whole curriculum. For example, the same concepts will need to be presented in many different ways. Children's learning is not subject-based, but we must ensure that we are providing a breadth of curriculum and this will need to be carefully planned. In the early years, much of the curriculum can be provided through setting up a variety of areas within the classroom which are permanently available, such as the home corner, construction area, creative area, and a writing and graphics area. Each area should have a breadth of learning built into it. The home corner, for example, will need to be planned in such a way as to ensure that mathematical, language and literacy, geographical, historical and social learning can take place. A specific science area may be set up with equipment and interesting objects for children to explore, but specific scientifically-focused activities will also need to be planned. The use of broad themes and topics which are relevant to the children are also a useful tool in planning. *Outdoor provision,* so important for all young children as it is one of the best environments for learning, will also need to be planned to ensure coverage of the breadth of the curriculum. Outdoor provision needs to incorporate all areas of learning. The outdoor environment can be used to provide quite *different* learning opportunities to what is possible inside – for example, running, climbing or digging in the garden. However, learning opportunities *similar* to what can happen inside can also be provided on a much larger scale – for example, drawing with chalks on the ground or experiments with water and sand. These can give children much needed **physically active** first-hand experiences.

Both indoor and outdoor provision should be planned using the QCA's six areas of learning for the Foundation Stage (1999). Using these as a basis for planning will ensure that there is breadth of experience provided for the children. The Early Learning Goals and related curriculum guidance (QCA, 2000) place a strong emphasis on the importance of children's social and emotional development and language development. Even though the Foundation Stage areas of learning have different titles, all of the National Curriculum subject areas are covered – and a great deal more – allowing for a smooth transition into the National Curriculum programmes of study as well as the National Literacy and Numeracy Strategies.

A distinction between work and play?

Early years teachers know that play is an important means of learning, although they are also aware that it is not always seen as such by parents or teachers of older children. All the great theorists and practitioners upon which we base our understanding of how children learn emphasise the importance of play to learning. Play is often seen as what children choose for themselves to do, rather than what teachers organise for them. However, its importance for learning means that it must be as carefully planned for as teacher-directed activities. For children in reception classes, play needs to remain of equal importance as it is in the nursery. The QCA and DFEE stress the value of play throughout the Foundation Stage and acknowledge that it takes a vital role in children's learning. However, although the QCA Guidance gives some advice on how the curriculum should be taught, it mainly gives general guidance based on principles of good quality early years education. It is the responsibility of the teacher to teach in the best possible way, which means taking the role of play in learning seriously.

Teachers need to be just as involved in children's play as they are in anything else that goes on in the classroom and outdoor space. The child needs to take the lead, but it is the adult who provides the 'scaffolding', to use Bruner's terminology, or the support the child will need in learning something new – whether this is social, physical, attitudinal, a process skill, or a concept. In order for play to enable the child to operate at her/his highest level, as Vygotsky suggests, it needs to be resourced thoughtfully, and for staff to become involved. Play is as important a part of what teachers assess as anything else. Just as teachers need to observe all the other activities they set up, they also need to observe play in order to look for significant achievement.

Example: A group of four year olds playing with dough. One child, who had recently had a birthday, takes a lump of dough and turns it into a 'birthday cake' by placing some dough knives vertically into it. Another child suggests they offer it to other children and a discussion ensues about parties. The teacher, observing this, then asks if she can join in. She suggests the need for invitations and the children find card, pens and envelopes; after a discussion on what to write, the teacher encourages them all to try out their own writing. Play continues for a considerable time, with all the children able to contribute and use their knowledge about parties, writing, making telephone calls and a sign for the home corner door, discussions about time, finding the right size of clothes, making paper plates and decorations, and preparing some more dough 'food'. By the end the teacher had managed to note down what she felt were significant achievements for several of the six children involved, each of which she discussed with them later on, after the play had finished. For one this was a process skill in writing, for another a physical skill in cutting, for another an attitude development in relation to confidence. The following day the children wanted to continue the play, and this time were able to do so without her involvement. For one child in particular this was very significant to his attitude and social development, as he managed to sustain a role in group play without becoming frustrated for longer than ever before.

During this play the children were developing their literacy and language skills, their physical skills, their mathematical, scientific and technological understanding and skills, as well as their social skills. Planning and organisation in nursery and reception classes need to ensure that the curriculum is presented in a meaningful way, such as that described above, to all the children. This kind of play is one way to provide the *meaningful context* which Donaldson discusses. It reflects their own experiences and builds on these.

Developing reflectiveness

It is important that right from the beginning of their educational careers children are helped to be made aware of their own achievements, and to reflect on their learning. Ensuring this is taking place means incorporating a dialogue with children about their learning into daily classroom practice. This may seem easier said than done, especially with the younger children and those less verbally competent. It is important that children are not *pressurised* into answering the teachers' questions, but that the possibility of a dialogue or conversation about their learning is begun. Sometimes the initial attempts made by the teacher might be met by a shrug of the shoulders, but once it becomes an established pattern and the teacher has worked out the best way to approach each child, the dividends will be evident. Soon you are likely to find that the children will be initiating the 'assessment dialogue' with you.

Creating a climate for learning

All staff working with young children need to be sensitive towards them as individuals, willing to give time to listen to them, however competently they can communicate. By gathering information from those who know them best – their parents/carers – staff can begin to build on their experiences, interests, knowledge and understanding. For significant achievement to take place for all children, creating a climate in school in which *all* children are valued is essential. This means valuing their individuality, their interests, skills and knowledge. It means showing that each child's personal and cultural background is valued and welcome. It means having high expectations of every child, knowing her/his capabilities through observing, discussing these observations, then building on them.

Creating the best learning environment means:

◆ **acknowledging the importance of a 'settling in' period.** All children need time to settle in and adjust to school or nursery. Making sure that routines are explained and that they know what is expected of them is an important part of this.

◆ **allowing for flexibility in what is planned** to allow children to be involved in different ways and at different levels. This means open-ended activities, events and tasks, but it does *not* mean being vague about planning. Learning intentions need to be carefully thought out for all provision, whether it is the water or sand tray, the home corner or a specific science activity, but they need to allow for differentiation.

◆ **listening to children**, however relevant or irrelevant you may find their comments. What they say indicates not only their level of understanding but also their interests.

◆ **being sensitive to children's needs** and giving support where it is necessary. This means observing children and having discussions with parents as well as the child.

◆ **being aware of possible inequalities** in access for all children to the breadth of the curriculum. This means evaluating what is going on to ensure that boys or girls are not dominating one particular area or kind of provision, and acting to change this. It is also important to make sure that children new to learning English or children from different ethnic groups are not being excluded by others in some way.

◆ **making learning intentions explicit.** Early years teachers are not always used to making learning intentions explicit to young children. The emphasis on breadth in the curriculum and differentiation in early childhood education has often meant that specific learning intentions the teacher has for individual children are sometimes not made clear to the child, but remain in the teacher's head. This does not enable the child either to develop a reflectiveness about their own learning or to strive to extend their learning. Making these clear to the child is most likely to get the desired results.

◆ **making sure the learning environment and resources are attractively and invitingly presented.** This can help to make the curriculum explicit and visible to the child.
◆ **ensuring that time to observe** while participating in the children's activities is built into planning and organisation.
◆ **planning for a mixture of teaching styles** so that individual, paired, small group and large group types of activities are planned, in which children can either be independent or staff can be involved.
◆ **the role of the teacher and support staff** is sometimes to lead, offering attainable and meaningful challenges, and at other times to be led by the child as support and companion.

Significant achievement in the early years

What does it mean in Nursery and Reception classes?

This book focuses on significant achievement in all areas of learning and development for children in nursery and reception classes. Assessing significant achievement under all the headings highlighted in Chapter 1 is a very helpful way to examine the nature of the learning that has taken place. Physical skills, social skills, attitude development, process skills and concept development all form a part of the learning in every area of the early years curriculum.

When we talk about recording significant achievement, we are not looking at each little step on the road to development that every child in the class takes – this would make the assessment and record-keeping task too arduous to be of any use: most of the time would be spent in record-keeping, without time left to consider its significance or to teach! What we are looking for is 'leaps' that children take in their development; the important steps which move a child forward to something new. Often the teacher will need to organise to look for these by observing and noting down her observations as she is working with the children. Some examples of this have already been given in Chapter 1 and show what this can mean for different children. Chapter 3 provides many more.

It is important to be aware that what is significant for one child will not necessarily be significant for another:

Mark and James started nursery at the same time and often play imaginatively together. Mark often chooses to write and draw alone, writing his name and combinations of other letters he knows how to write. To observe Mark writing in chalk on the ground outside, when going on an imaginary journey, is not a significant achievement for him as he often uses his writing to convey messages. However, for James, who shares an equal role in the game, picking up a pencil which he holds in a fist grip, making some tentative marks on the paper which he hands to Mark, saying 'That's where we go' as he climbs on the vehicle they have made, is very significant. This was a significant achievement for him – both physical and conceptual- as it was the first time he had tried to write a message; and when later asked about it, it was clear he was beginning to understand that marks on paper can convey a meaning. In this area James will need a lot more significant steps before he will be able to form letters correctly, using a correct pencil grip. For Mark, however, the next significant achievements will be when he begins to make the connection between letter sound and letter in his writing (concept), as well as to include children other than James into his play and to take turns without adult support.

For Sadiya and Rebecca what constitutes significant achievements are also very different. They were both piling blocks into carts to transport them in order to build a house. Rebecca was, as usual, taking the lead in the play, telling the story and making the decisions. However, the way she had piled up the blocks had meant that she could not move her cart without them falling out. Sadiya, on the other hand, had loaded hers symmetrically, showing her understanding of shape and space (mathematical concepts), while Rebecca became increasingly frustrated. The teacher intervened and asked Sadiya to show her friend how she had managed to transport her blocks so successfully. The fact that Sadiya was able to do this, which meant explaining what she had done and beginning to take a leading role in the play herself, was very significant for Sadiya (in terms of both attitude development and process skills). The significant achievement took place for Rebecca when she managed to make a well balanced and symmetrical building with blocks another day.

Highlighting a child's significant achievements and using these for individual planning will result in much more effective planning for every child than the 'hit and miss' often experienced when only using methods of planning which focus on the class or group as a whole.

Possible lines of development

Outlining some possible lines of development for children in their early years may help to illustrate the meaning of the five aspects of learning – *physical skills*, *social skills*, *attitude development*, *'concept clicking'* and *process skills* – across the range of the early years curriculum and into Key Stage 1.

I have chosen to look at this under one broad area of learning and experience – **creative development**. This area of development covers children's exploration and experimentation with two- and three-dimensional materials and a range of tools (brushes, pencils, scissors, etc), and their ability to interpret and represent their knowledge, experience and imagination with these; their ability to select the appropriate tools and handle them, and use a range of different techniques; their developing imaginations and involvement in imaginative play; and their interest in and ability to explore, perform, and express themselves through music, drama and dance. It is about being creative in all these ways and responding to the creations and creativity of others. In terms of curriculum 'subjects' it can be seen that this area of development incorporates a wide range of 'subjects' – in fact it is difficult to see which would be left out! However, for children beyond the reception class some elements in the National Curriculum programmes of study for art, design and technology, music, English, physical education and most probably science and maths would be covered.

What follows are just a few examples of likely lines of development in this area. They are not comprehensive, and many children's achievements will fall outside the boundaries made here.

Physical skills

FROM holding pencil in fist and making marks on paper
TO making representations from imagination or real objects including some detail.

FROM holding scissors in two hands to make cuts on edge of paper
TO cutting out own drawing accurately.

FROM building a simple tower in blocks
TO making an imaginative and symmetrical model with many features.

FROM making simple repeated movements in dance
TO using a range of movements appropriately to convey different ideas.

Social skills

FROM playing/working alone or in parallel with others
TO being able to work/play collaboratively in a small group.

FROM taking on one role in a pair or small group (eg leader)
TO being able to take on a range of roles.

FROM talking to one staff member
TO being able to talk to a group of children and other adults.

FROM expressing needs and desires and simple observations to adults
TO holding an extended conversation and expressing ideas on a topic with an adult or other child.

Attitude development

FROM needing adult support and help
TO doing some things alone.

FROM quick exploration of some of the creative activities
and resources available
TO a concentrated period of time involved in these
activities.

FROM being dependent on adult to suggest activities
TO making independent choices.

FROM being unsure of how to use some materials, tools and
techniques
TO being confident in how to use them.

FROM adult drawing child's attention to qualities in visual
appearance, sound, movements, patterns
TO observing these for self and talking about them.

FROM silent exploration
TO being able to talk about intentions or what has been
done.

FROM staying with activity for short period
TO being able to concentrate for longer and persist in
problem-solving independently.

Concept development

FROM spreading glue on boxes/paper but not using it to
fasten materials together
TO understanding that there are a variety of ways of joining
materials which are used for different materials and
purposes.

FROM spreading paint on paper at random
TO understanding that a pattern or representation can be
made using a range of techniques.

FROM knowing that an object is 'big' or 'little'
TO knowing that size has different dimensions – height,
length, width, etc.

FROM attempting to balance objects at random
TO understanding that larger objects need to go underneath
smaller ones.

FROM banging a range of percussion instruments in the same way
TO understanding that different actions can produce different kinds of sounds.

Process skills

FROM placing junk materials together at random
TO being able to make simple representations, using a variety of materials and methods of joining.

FROM needing adult support to use a range of skills and techniques
TO being able to show another child how to do something.

FROM playing imaginatively alone in the home corner/with transport toys/etc
TO developing a sustained story line for others to follow.

FROM building a simple vertical tower with a construction set
TO following a simple plan.

FROM following a simple plan devised by others
TO being able to draw own plan for construction model.

FROM repeating an action on percussion instruments
TO being able to discriminate between different sounds and talk about these.

FROM joining in with well-known ring games
TO being able to appreciate and talk about a dance sequence created by other children.

Ideally, we want the children in our classes to be confident with others in a group situation; confident in what they can achieve and have already achieved; confident to attempt to solve their own problems and work independently; confident enough to ask questions and to begin to investigate ideas alone and with others. This is why attitude and social skills are so important when looking for significant achievements, as these form the background to all learning. Those working with children in the early years are very aware of the importance of the process rather than the product – a tangible object or 'creation' which is often unimportant to the child. Concepts are important because once a concept has 'clicked' into place it can be transferred to a new situation and become of general use to the child. However, it must be remembered that there are many stages in learning any concept. And finally, without physical control over one's own movements and actions, it is not possible to 'act' – and without action little can happen.

Creating the conditions for significant achievement to occur

The approach to teaching outlined so far should ensure not only that significant achievement can occur for all children but also that it can be seen and acknowledged when it does occur. However, it is worth reiterating some of the conditions which are necessary here.

Observing

First, we need to look for significant achievement in all the learning experiences that take place in school – in the classroom and outdoor space. In order to be able to recognise it when it does occur, we must know what the possibilities are within the learning activities and the environment we have created. Clarifying these for ourselves, the other staff we work with and ultimately for the children means being aware of the learning potential within an area. Often it is when a child approaches something in a different way, or makes a comment which surprises us, that we are made aware of possibilities we had never previously thought of.

Planning

We need to make sure that our system of planning incorporates a cycle whereby assessments highlight the specific experiences a child needs next, and ensure that these are incorporated into future plans.

Talking with the parents

We need to open up a two-way dialogue with parents to ensure they are aware of what achievements are happening, and to make sure they can inform us about a child's achievements at home.

Talking with the children

By talking with children about what they are doing and learning, we can begin to understand a lot more about their achievements as well as helping them to become more reflective and aware of their own learning. When we have seen something which we believe is significant for the child, we need to talk to the child about this in an open way, so that she/he can tell us, in her/his own way, *why* it happened. This helps us in planning for the 'right' next stage and helps the child to move towards it.

Time to review

We need to make a time to review with children what they have been doing during a morning or afternoon. Sometimes this can be done in a group situation and at other times with smaller numbers of children or even individually. This will help children to consider for themselves what they have been doing and learning, what their interests are, and ultimately to be more aware of what they don't like doing and why.

Certain management procedures need to be in place in every classroom for staff to be able to work in greater depth over longer periods of time with even the youngest classful of children. This means making sure that children can be independent in the way they use all provision and that they are shown how to respect and look after all the equipment they use, as well as each other and the general learning environment. Once children are settled in and understand the routines and expectations of school, the youngest of children enjoy the sense of responsibility of being independent and caring for their environment. It also allows the staff to become participant observers, looking for significant achievement.

From the Foundation Stage to the National Curriculum

Continuity in learning is essential if children are to achieve their full potential in school. The broad curriculum framework (the six areas of learning) referred to in this chapter for children in their early years leads smoothly into the National Curriculum for all the subjects in Year 1. Often, elements within the programmes of study will have already been achieved by some of the children in reception classes.

As the areas of learning in the Foundation Stage are broader than the National Curriculum subjects, schools which have mixed reception and Year 1 classes should have no problems with planning using a mixture of both the 'areas' and programmes of study. The two main differences between the National Curriculum and Foundation Stage are Personal, Social and Emotional development and Knowledge and Understanding of the World. Personal, Social and Emotional development could be planned for all the children, as it is as relevant for Year 1 children as it is for reception. The best approach for Knowledge and Understanding of the World would be to split it up into its constituent components of science, technology, history, geography and ICT.

Within any age group a wide range of abilities is likely to exist. However, both the National Curriculum and the Foundation Stage areas of learning are designed to allow for a full range of abilities to be taught. The Early Learning Goals are a guide to where most children should be by the end of the reception year. The Level Descriptions for each Attainment Target in the National Curriculum are only to be used to assess the children's level of attainment at the *end* of each Key Stage. So, for Key Stage 1 these do not affect children until the end of Year 2, when *'teachers should judge which description best fits the pupil's performance'*.

However, it is tracking children's significant achievement from the very beginning which is most likely to ensure progression in every child's learning. This is then used to decide what specific experiences a child needs next within the broader curriculum planning. Tracking significant achievement means noting the important steps in a child's development across the curriculum. It does not mean collecting evidence of everything the child does. The examples of significant achievement in Chapter 3 are actual examples collected by teachers in nursery and reception classes and are reproduced in this book to help illustrate what significant achievements look like for children in this age group.

3 Significant Achievement in Action

We have so far discussed the kind of conditions that need to be created to help ensure that significant achievement will occur for every child in the early years classroom. The next step is to observe and record it. To make this possible, two processes need to be incorporated into the normal daily life of the class – looking for achievements and thinking about their significance. None of this should be difficult or take up valuable extra time in or out of school hours, though like any system it will need to be organised and monitored regularly. Suggestions for how to introduce and operate the new approach to assessment are discussed in detail in Chapter 6. However, the intention is that the achievement should be recorded at the time it happens, with the child present, wherever possible.

The rest of this chapter presents a wide range of examples of significant achievement collected by staff in nursery classes, nursery schools and reception classes. These examples not only cover many curriculum areas, but also cover the different aspects of learning already discussed. As you will see, often within one example of significant achievement several aspects of learning, and sometimes several curriculum areas (see the example of Rowena, for instance), form part of the achievement.

A standard format for analysing each example has been used in all of the books in this series, and this helps to ensure continuity between the different phases of education. We recommend you adopt this format, as it clarifies speedily what learning took place and, most importantly, why. The format is as follows:

◆ **What did the child do?**
◆ **Why was it significant?**
◆ **Why did it happen?** *(child's view, and/or teacher's view)*

◆ **Type of achievement** (*attitude, social, physical, process or concept*)
◆ **Teaching implications**

For each child, the example quoted is not an isolated event. It is part of a record of achievement and progress, and the achievement has depended on some previous experience, teaching or opportunity made available to the child. The examples have been organised by age, to draw attention to the breadth of possible achievement for each age.

THREE YEAR OLDS

Social development

David, *3 years 9 months*

After looking at the new photo-book about himself, with his mother and a member of staff, David said goodbye to his mother enthusiastically and cheerfully went to join some other children at an activity.

Why was it significant?

This was the first time David said goodbye to his mother enthusiastically, without getting upset and imploring her to stay.

Why did this happen?

Teacher's view: The previous day, David had helped his teacher to make a photo-book about what he enjoys in nursery and about saying goodbye to his mother. As he came in today, this was shown to him and his mother. **Child's view:** *'I feel happy now. I want to show the book to my Dad and my Nan.'*

Type of achievement: social skill

Comment and teaching implications

This child had found it difficult to part from his mother since he first started in the nursery. Staff had tried several different strategies to ease the situation, and this one was paying off. A follow-up to this might be to remind him it was easy to say goodbye; to ask him to help in the production of individual resources about other children too; and to invite him to make his own book about himself.

Anna, *3 years 6 months*

While mixing paints, Anna happily handed out pots to other children and was able to take turns mixing and filling pots with another child. She was also able to wait for her turn at the woodwork bench.

Why was it significant?

On both occasions Anna was able to take turns without a conflict, and with only one request from a staff member.

Why did it happen?

Child's view: *'We have to share'* (said to another child on both occasions).

Type of achievement: social skill

Comment and teaching implications

The social rules were made very clear by staff from the beginning of these activities. (Make sure social rules are made equally clear in less structured areas of provision.)

Language: Reading

Marianne, *3 years 8 months*

On the computer Marianne recognised all the initial letters of the names of her family members and named them 'H for Harry', etc.

Why was it significant?

This was the first time Marianne had shown such letter recognition: previously she had recognised only her own initials.

Why did it happen?

Child's view: *'Cos my Mum was showing me.'*

Type of achievement: concept development

Comment and teaching implications

Although the catalyst had been writing with her mother at home, the writing area at the nursery had also been significant in drawing Marianne's attention to the alphabet, and displays including the names of children and other family members' names. A follow-up will be to continue a dialogue with her mother about what she does at home; and to introduce Marianne to other initial letters, e.g. friends' initials.

Language: Writing

Natalie, *3 years 2 months*

Natalie wrote her name on her painting (as a zigzag line).

Why was it significant?

This was the first time she had done so.

Why did it happen?

Child's view: *'I done my name.'*
Teacher's view: She watched another child write his name – peer influence.

Type of achievement: concept development

Comment and teaching implications

It was staff encouraging children to try and write their own names on their work which brought about this achievement. As the teacher's comment shows, watching another child also helped here. The teaching implications will be to congratulate her and encourage her to write her own name every time and, when appropriate, to show her the similarities between the letter N and a zigzag.

Amy, *3 years 11 months*

Whilst playing with small world toys, another child said *'They all have to leave the park now – it's closed.'* When her teacher suggested writing a sign saying 'Park Closed', to go on the gate, Amy said *'I'll do it.'* The only support needed was the teacher helping her to sound it out. She then wrote *'ThE PC E PA OP'* independently and read it out: *'The park is open'*.

Why was it significant?

This was the first time Amy had tried to do so much independent writing.

Why did it happen?

Child's view: *'I just know now. I just do it.'*
Teacher's view: She was motivated by her involvement in the play.

Type of achievement: process skill, concept development, attitude development

Comment and teaching implications

Amy had been helped by staff over the previous months to make phonic connections with the letters she could write. The next step will be to encourage her to try and sound words out for herself.

Stephen, *3 years 9 months*

Stephen wrote his name really clearly on his picture.

Why was it significant?

Stephen knows the letters of his name, but has difficulties in holding pencils.

Why did this happen?

Child's view: *'Cos I was trying really hard.'* His mother says he has been practising with his brother all holiday.

Type of achievement: **physical development**

Comment and teaching implications

At nursery Stephen had also been supported in his fine motor development by being encouraged to use a range of mark-making tools. This will need to continue, along with offering activities such as sewing and threading, as well as encouraging his writing at home and at nursery.

Mathematics

Michelle, *3 years 2 months*

Michelle picked up a triangle (percussion) and asked what it was. Then every time she saw a triangle shape around the nursery, she came back to tell the teacher or asked what shape it was.

Why was it significant?

Michelle's interest in shape resulted in new learning. She was able to involve a member of staff in following her interest.

Why did it happen?

Teacher's view: Michelle is a new child who now feels confident enough in her relationship to initiate an activity with her teacher.

Type of achievement: **concept development** and **social skill**

Comment

In order to help the new children to settle in, the staff spend time with each new child in small-group situations. They had also made up some games about shape. This helped to develop the child's awareness of shape, as well as build up her confidence with her teacher.

Janine, *3 years 6 months*

Janine counted the number of books she had picked up. She first counted 1, 3, 2, then said *'No, 1, 2, 3, 4.'*

Why was it significant?

Janine was able to self-correct her counting.

Why did it happen?

Child's view: *'I can carry lots and lots.'*

Type of achievement: **process skill** and **attitude development**

Comment and teaching implications

The staff will have been reinforcing her counting skills in many activities. The next step will be to help her to learn new numbers and to count further.

Knowledge & understanding of the world

Charmaine, *3 years 6 months*

When told the paddling pool was not out because of the weather, Charmaine said: *'But when the clouds have blown away it will be blue sky and then it will be hot-hot-hot.'*

Why was it significant?

Charmaine was able to describe cause and effect very clearly.

Why did it happen?

Teacher's view: This was an informal conversation, where Charmaine was given time to talk.

Type of achievement: concept development

Comment and teaching implications

It is important for staff to encourage children to develop and give their own explanations for things. Often this will mean holding back on answering the 'why' questions children may ask, and getting them to express their own answers. It will also mean asking children open questions, such as *'I wonder what if...'*.

Creative development

Rita, *3 years 6 months*

Rita drew a picture, holding her pen in a pincer grip, whilst recounting a story about her mother. When she had finished, she said the drawing was of her mother.

Why was it significant?

This was the first time Rita had drawn with the pen held correctly and had talked about what she had drawn.

Why did it happen?

Teacher's view: Rita had been encouraged to draw by a member of staff who stayed with her. She was also aware of other children talking about their drawings.

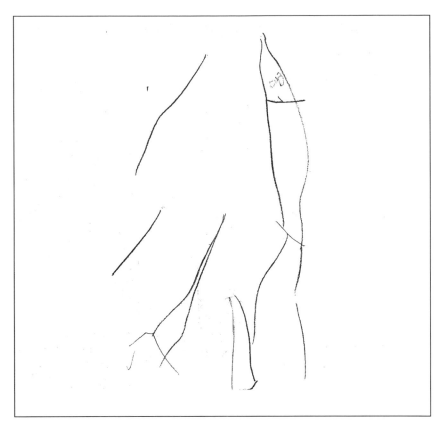

Rita's picture of her mother

Type of achievement: physical skill, social skill and concept development

Comment and teaching implications

This was an informal activity rather than a task with a set goal. The next step will be to encourage her to draw in this way more frequently, staying with her to encourage talk and to build up fine motor control.

Comment and teaching implications

Through observing Alan at play, staff were aware of his nervousness about climbing and how he usually avoided it. He had therefore been encouraged and supported by staff staying nearby while he tried. They will still need to continue encouraging him to try out other new things.

Language: Reading

Rashida, *4 years 3 months*

Rashida read the whole of *Whatever Next* to the teacher, not just relying on memory, context or picture cues, but actually breaking down words into constituent parts.

Why was it significant?

The staff have been aware of her writing skills at this level for some time, but this was the first time she had read in this way (at school).

Why did it happen?

Child's view: *'I wanted to do that.'*
Teacher's view: Rashida's comment indicates an attitude development.

Type of achievement: concept development and attitude development

Comment and teaching implications

The help and support Rashida has been given in her writing has had an effect on her skills and understanding in reading. Asking her to read in a relaxed one-to-one situation made her feel confident enough for this achievement to happen. The next step will be to make time for Rashida to read to a member of staff every day, and encourage her to read to other children too.

Language: Writing

Michael, *4 years 4 months*

Jack and
the beanstalk

by Michael

This is a
happy giant
who was chasing
Jack because he wants
Jack to stay for the
night in the castle.

Michael's 'giant story'

Encouraged by the teacher, Michael drew pictures and dictated a story. At first he did not understand what was meant. His teacher was unsure if he had understood that what he said could be written down.

Why was it significant?

This was the first time Michael engaged in story-telling. On previous occasions, when his friends had been involved in this kind of activity, Michael had found something else to do.

Why did it happen?

Child's view: At first Michael said he didn't know what to do, then decided to draw a giant. Said he knew the 'giant story'.

Type of achievement: **concept development** and **process skill**

Comment and teaching implications

It may have been that the situation of working alone with a member of staff gave him more confidence to try out something new. The next step will be to encourage him to develop these skills in other situations too.

Language: Speaking & listening

Catherine, *4 years 3 months*

Catherine was able to express her needs and describe simply what she was doing. While playing in the sand with a very small group and a member of staff, she said: *'I make a triangle'*, *'This is the cake.'* Talk was directed at a staff member.

Why was it significant?

Catherine has only recently begun to use sentences and she has not described what she is doing to this extent before, preferring to use gesture than words.

Why did it happen?

Teacher's view: It was a very small, quiet group; the adult was also listening rather than talking and Catherine obviously felt at ease.

Type of achievement: **attitude development** and **process skill**

Comment and teaching implications

Catherine has received a lot of language modelling in one-to-one situations from staff. It will be important now as a result of the achievement quoted here not to accept the use of gestures alone from her in small-group situations. Providing small-group situations for her will need to continue, as well as encouraging her to address talk to peers.

Mathematics

Louis, *4 years 2 months*

Louis found some grid paper in the writing area and drew a pattern using all of the paper, making rows of squares, each row a different colour. He said *'Look you can make squares with these dots.'*

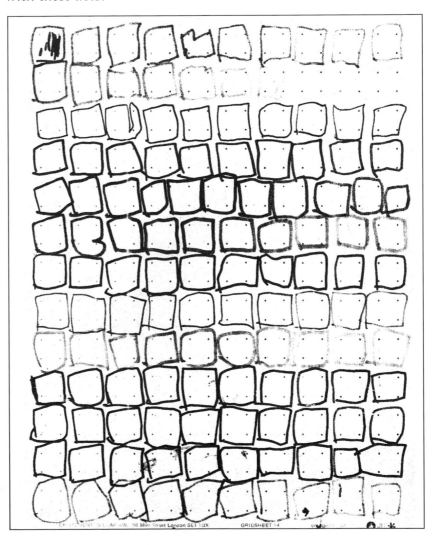

Why was it significant?

Louis had shown his awareness of shapes and shape names before, but had never made a pattern in this way.

Why did it happen?

Child's view: *'I thought about all the colours of the rainbow and I just drawed around four dots.'*

Type of achievement: concept development and process skill

Comment and teaching implications

The context for this development was several previous discussions between the staff and children about shape. The example of significant achievement shows the importance of leaving a range of equipment available (not just plain paper) for children's use. The next step for Louis could be to follow his interest in pattern by asking him to try making repeating patterns with different shapes and different materials, and to involve others with him in these activities.

Jade, *4 years 5 months*

Jade played turn-taking game, counted dice correctly and helped others to do so, moved her counter correctly and took turns without being reminded.

Why was it significant?

Jade carried out all the elements required in using this turn-taking game correctly and well.

Why did it happen?

Child's view: *'I like that game.'*

Type of achievement: social skill and process skill

Comment and teaching implications

The teacher's role in allowing the children to take the lead in organising the game was significant here, as well as the group of children chosen to play the game. The next step will be to offer the same group more complex games.

Knowledge & understanding of the world

Billy, *4 years 4 months*

When encouraged to mix his own colours, Billy at first needed some support, then decided he wanted to make orange and realised he needed yellow. He persisted in spite of having no yellow paint, mixing in different colours methodically and predicting what colour might result each time.

Why was it significant?

Billy tends not to persist with something new. He was also able to demonstrate his knowledge about colour and develop this further.

Why did it happen?

Child's view: *'I want orange colour cos I'm painting for my mum and she likes orange.'*

Type of achievement: attitude development, process skills and concept development

Comment and teaching implications

A link with home was significant here as a motivating reason for persistence, as well as the teacher's role in encouraging Billy to experiment. Both of these aspects will be important issues to address in future planning for Billy.

Jamal, *4 years 8 months*

Jamal made an electric circuit independently, with two bulbs. As it wasn't bright enough, he tried to solve the problem by taking it outside and putting it in the tunnel. He talked about it *'still not working'*.

Why was it significant?

Jamal was trying to solve his problem by himself.

Why did it happen?

Teacher's view: Jamal had been interested in some of the resources left available to children, especially the illustrated reference books on electric circuits.

Type of achievement: **attitude development** and **concept development**

Comment and teaching implications

This child had been involved in carefully planned and well-resourced teacher-led activities with circuits. Leaving the resources available with visual support – plans of circuits, illustrated reference books – was important in encouraging the child to explore by himself. Jamal will need help to solve the problem he has identified – his teacher will need to help him carry out some tests on the circuit itself.

Creative development

Rowena, *4 years*

This was the first time Rowena had joined a music session; first she played piano whilst others sang for a few moments, then wandered off. When she heard the teacher playing *The Wheels on the Bus*, she came back, found four chairs, asked others to sit in them, put a doll in an empty chair, and collected small pieces of paper for tickets and buttons for money.

Why was it significant?

On other occasions Rowena had shown no interest in music sessions, and was usually absorbed in imaginative play alone. She demonstrated her ability to organise play for others, and be creative, as well as her understanding of one-to-one correspondence.

Why did it happen?

No comment from the child.

Type of achievement: **social skill**, **concept development** and **process skill**

Comment and teaching implications

Rowena was given the freedom to move in and out of the music session. This allowed her to use it creatively and to involve others in this. The next step will be to encourage her to become more involved in group sessions, by allowing her to bring her own interests to these and helping her to participate in the other children's ideas too.

FIVE YEAR OLDS

Language: Speaking & listening

Dean, *5 years 3 months*

Dean was able to explain the dinner-time routine very clearly to another younger child, explaining why some things happened. He then said he would like to look after the younger child at dinner time.

Why was it significant?

Dean had not shown this attitude before, or given such detailed explanations.

Why did it happen?

Child's view: *'I know what you have to do and he's new.'*

Type of achievement: **attitude development**, **social skill** and **process skill**

Comment and teaching implications

This significant achievement happened for Dean because the children here are encouraged by the teacher to look after each other. Dean saw the needs of a younger child and realised he could use his skills and knowledge here. This was a child who does not usually take on an organising role in groups.

A page from one of Sita's pop-up books

Why did it happen?

Child's view: *'It was the pop-up books.'*
Teacher's view: Sita had been very interested in some new pop-up books which had just arrived.

Type of achievement: attitude development and process skill

Comment and teaching implications

Providing interesting and unusual resources here acted as the catalyst to moving Sita forward to take a significant leap in persistence. The teacher will need to continue to provide a wide range of books for the class, and to think of other inventive ways of presenting writing tasks for the children.

John, *5 years 6 months*

John wrote a story and illustrated it, based on a book he had enjoyed listening to, *On the Way Home*. He then read his story to the whole class.

Type of achievement: social skill, concept development and process skill

Comment and teaching implications

Rowena was given the freedom to move in and out of the music session. This allowed her to use it creatively and to involve others in this. The next step will be to encourage her to become more involved in group sessions, by allowing her to bring her own interests to these and helping her to participate in the other children's ideas too.

FIVE YEAR OLDS

Language: Speaking & listening

Dean, *5 years 3 months*

Dean was able to explain the dinner-time routine very clearly to another younger child, explaining why some things happened. He then said he would like to look after the younger child at dinner time.

Why was it significant?

Dean had not shown this attitude before, or given such detailed explanations.

Why did it happen?

Child's view: *'I know what you have to do and he's new.'*

Type of achievement: attitude development, social skill and process skill

Comment and teaching implications

This significant achievement happened for Dean because the children here are encouraged by the teacher to look after each other. Dean saw the needs of a younger child and realised he could use his skills and knowledge here. This was a child who does not usually take on an organising role in groups.

Language: Reading

Anne Marie, *5 years 2 months*

Anne Marie was asked to retell a favourite story to her teacher and one other child, and chose *Three Billy Goats Gruff*. At first she said she couldn't, so the other child began. Anne Marie said *'No, that's wrong'*, then took over, telling the story well with the aid of the book, lots of use of book language and expression, and telling the story in correct sequence.

Why was it significant?

This was the first time Anne Marie had been confident enough to do this.

Why did it happen?

Teacher's view: The paired situation was good for building up her confidence, especially when she realised she knew the story better than the other child.

Type of achievement: **process skill** and **attitude development**

Comment and teaching implications

This example shows the importance of arranging different social contexts in the classroom. The achievement would have been unlikely either in an individual session with the teacher or in a larger group. The next step will be to continue to get her to work in paired situations with another quiet child, and to show her where the phrases she uses from the texts appear on the page.

Aaron, *5 years 11 months*

Having just arrived in this country, Aaron does not speak English yet and was looking at books quietly alone. His teacher noticed his interest, and read *Not Now, Bernard* to him, making sure he understood the text by translating one or two words. Aaron then took the book and read it back to her, remembering the repeating lines, and looking to teacher for confirmation. He read the word 'ate' as a

Portuguese word, realised that it didn't make sense and translated the word correctly into Portuguese.

Why was it significant?

This was the first time Aaron had read anything in English, and was able to read for meaning and translate.

Why did it happen?

Child's view: (in Portuguese) *'I want to speak English too.'*
Teacher's view: He was motivated by a strong desire to be accepted into the class group.

Type of achievement: concept development, process skill and attitude development

Comment and teaching implications

The one-to-one situation with the teacher was significant here, even though the child's motivation was to be accepted into the class group. It will be important for the teacher to build on this successful event, presenting him with a range of simple story books with strong visuals to read with him; involving him in activities in very small groups, making sure he has visual support and can understand, and giving him essential vocabulary for social interaction with peers.

Language: Writing

Sita, *5 years 8 months*

Sita made four pop-up books about monsters (see over), putting dots where the pages had to be turned.

Why was it significant?

Although capable of this level of work, Sita usually does not persist in this way.

A page from one of Sita's pop-up books

Why did it happen?

Child's view: *'It was the pop-up books.'*
Teacher's view: Sita had been very interested in some new pop-up books which had just arrived.

Type of achievement: **attitude development** and **process skill**

Comment and teaching implications

Providing interesting and unusual resources here acted as the catalyst to moving Sita forward to take a significant leap in persistence. The teacher will need to continue to provide a wide range of books for the class, and to think of other inventive ways of presenting writing tasks for the children.

John, *5 years 6 months*

John wrote a story and illustrated it, based on a book he had enjoyed listening to, *On the Way Home*. He then read his story to the whole class.

Why was it significant?

This was the first time John had done this; he had used letters he knew how to form and, when he read it back, he used his memory of the original story to do so.

Why did this happen?

Child's view: *'It's lovely writing, it's all done.'*
Teacher's view: The fantasy in the book really inspired him.

Type of achievement: **concept development, process skill** and **attitude development**

Comment and teaching implications

Using well-known and popular story books as a basis for children's own creative writing resulted in this achievement. The teacher will need to build on this, finding more highly imaginative stories like this, as well as helping John to make links between letters and sounds in his writing.

Mathematics

Christopher, *5 years 3 months*

A group were making a number frieze (1 – 20). Christopher decided to make 50. As he used a collage of match sticks, he found it difficult to keep count. Later, he managed to count 47 with help to remember the numbers 30 and 40. He then worked out on his fingers that he needed 3 more.

Why was it significant?

Christopher set himself a difficult challenge and persisted. He showed his understanding of number by counting on.

Why did it happen?

Child's view: *'I can do big numbers.'*

Type of achievement: **attitude development** and **concept development**

Comment and teaching implications

This teacher had seen the value of children making their *own* classroom displays. It gave the child an ideal opportunity to demonstrate his skills and presented him with a challenge. Next she will offer him more challenges using larger numbers; helping him to remember how to count in 10s; checking his numeral recognition and developing this.

Sally, *5 years 6 months*

Each child made their own survey on travel to school. Sally collected the information with another child and then wrote it up in a diagram. She added up numbers in each category without help, self-corrected her response, and could explain what the evidence showed.

Why was it significant?

This was the first time she had done a task like this without help.

Why did it happen?

Child's view: *'I like drawing cars and things. I counted it up.'*

Type of achievement: **process skill**

Comment and teaching implications

Although the teacher felt that the numeracy skills were the significant achievement here, the motivation, as can be seen by the child's response, was the opportunity to draw. When planning all kinds of learning activities, the teacher will need to take account of Sally's interest in drawing.

Knowledge & understanding of the world

Felicity, *5 years 4 months*

Felicity and others were asked to make a bridge and think of a way to test its strength. At first she was very unsure and had no idea how to start. Once started, she made great progress and built a strong and stable model.

Sally's 'travel to school' survey

Why was it significant?

Felicity is often reluctant to start an activity. Having been very unsure of herself at first, after a short discussion she gained confidence and persisted.

Why did it happen?

Teacher's view: The initial discussion helped her to feel confident.

Type of achievement: attitude development

Comment and teaching implications

The teacher is now aware that the reluctance to start an activity is related to lack of confidence. She will now help to build up Felicity's self-confidence by allowing her discussion time at the beginning of a problem-solving activity.

Creative development

James, *5 years 2 months*

Sitting next to another child who was cutting out a mask, James was able to cut across the paper, holding the scissors correctly in one hand. Only reassurance was needed this time.

Why was it significant?

It was the first time he had used scissors correctly without help.

Why did it happen?

Child's view: *'You hold them like this, don't you? I can do it, I want to make a mask too.'*

Type of achievement: physical skill, attitude development and social skill

Comment and teaching implications

Although motivated here by a new friendship with another child, James had also been given lots of help by staff with his fine motor skill development and encouraged to practise. Although he may still need some help with these skills, this example shows an important leap in confidence. The teacher will encourage James to continue to work with his new friend.

Examining the significant achievements for children across the age range which have been collected together here, you will notice how often **attitude development** appears as one aspect of the achievement. Usually it goes hand in hand with another aspect of development – often a process skill. Why should this be?

Much of the learning which constitutes an obvious step forward for a child requires a development of confidence, self-esteem or self-awareness or independence. Perhaps this is best related to Vygotsky's (1978) often quoted statement: *'What a child can do with assistance today, she will be able to do by herself tomorrow.'* The 'assistance' may have come from home, from other children or staff, but it is likely to have been a combination of these. However, it is the cumulative effect of the previous support plus the learning opportunities provided for the child which result in a leap in attitude as well as other skills or development – a leap to feeling and knowing, and sometimes even saying, *'I can do that now.'*

The **social situation** in which an achievement occurs is an important factor allowing an attitude development to happen. The social context may have meant that the child needs a lesser amount of staff support. This does not necessarily constitute an achievement in social development itself, but rather provides the necessary conditions for the achievement to take place. However, as will be seen from the comments and teaching implications highlighted in each example, this is often a crucial factor to be addressed in future planning.

4 Development across the Curriculum

This chapter highlights some of the stages a child is likely go through in her/his learning and development in nursery and reception class. It is usual to acknowledge that children of the same age may be at very different levels in their development in any particular area of learning, and teachers will plan accordingly. However, it is often assumed that all children learn the same things in the same way. But young children may vary considerably not only in their learning styles, but also in the routes they take in order to arrive at a similar stage of development. This may be due to, amongst other things, a difference in personal approach to learning, to different interests or to different experiences. But whatever the reasons, there are very important implications for teachers, because the experiences each child needs next to further her/his learning may differ considerably.

The best way of illustrating how development actually happens in practice is by using real examples of children developing over time:

Sarah has used her own form of writing in her play since she first came to nursery when she was 3 years 3 months. This meant writing letters, telephone messages, shopping lists, notes and other writing marks on her drawings. This she did whenever and wherever pens and paper were found available around the nursery. At 3 years 9 months she began to tell others what the writing said, but was not yet attempting to form letters. At 4 years 4 months her teacher began to show her how to form letters that were significant to her, without devaluing her own writing. By 4 years 8 months she was able to write many of the letters from her own name and her brother's name, and still continued to write long messages in her own writing. She has now understood that there is a common code of writing which it is necessary to use if anyone else is to read her writing. Over this period Sarah had developed her creative writing and is now adding to this a knowledge of letters and handwriting.

Robert*, on the other hand, came to nursery at 3 years 3 months already able to write most of his name in capital letters. This he would do on any drawing, painting or model. By 3 years 10 months he knew many of the capital letters of the alphabet by sight, and could write all of his own name properly as well as his sister's name and parents' names (in capitals). Unlike Sarah, he did not include writing in his imaginative play or attempt to make up stories, messages or captions even when staff offered to scribe these for him. Staff modelled writing for him in many situations and showed him many different purposes for writing. Gradually his views and concepts of writing developed to include some creative writing. By 4 years 8 months Robert's stage of understanding and process skills were quite similar to Sarah's, but they had clearly moved along very different paths.*

Both of these children needed to be offered different experiences and given support in different ways in order to have a firm grounding in what it takes to become a writer, because they began at the age of 3 with very different views and experiences of writing.

In this chapter the development of four children in the early years phase of education will be examined. The examples used here are based on observations of significant achievement at around the ages of 3 years 3 months, 4 years 6 months and 5 years 6 months. Although only selected areas of learning are looked at, under specific curriculum headings, these have been taken from records of achievement compiled from observations of the whole child. The selection drawn on here does not represent all that will need to be highlighted in terms of a child's overall development.

After each example there is a section on 'Implications for teaching'. These note some of the immediate actions the teacher felt would be useful for the child resulting from the specific observation noted and are in no way intended to be the *only* specific teaching which would take place for that child. This teaching would be incorporated into the normal future planning over the next few weeks.

The curriculum areas chosen are **language development**, **mathematical development**, some aspects of **creative development** and **knowledge and understanding of the world**. As in the rest of the book, attitude development, process skills, social and physical aspects of development as well as concept development are highlighted, thereby encompassing a holistic approach to learning within curriculum areas. The curriculum headings selected have been chosen for several reasons. They are areas of learning that are very important in early childhood education. Once children leave the reception class, language (English), maths and science form the core subjects of the National Curriculum. Creative development is very much a cross-curricular area of learning which is usually considered very important in a good early years curriculum. As well as encompassing art, drama, imaginative play, music and dance, it also includes the foundation of so much learning in language, literacy, maths, science and technology, so long as its provision incorporates a breadth of experiences.

The observations of the children were taken in normal early years classroom settings, where much of the curriculum, as already described elsewhere, is taught through providing a rich and carefully planned environment for play experiences, both with and independent of staff involvement. As will be seen, the observations were made in these play situations as well as in teacher-led and teacher-initiated activities.

The selected areas of learning

Language development refers to all aspects of a child's early development in English (and first language where this is different) – speaking and listening, mark-making and the development of writing, and early experiences of reading, stories and the world of books and other forms of writing.

Mathematical development refers to experiences and developing awareness of mathematical ideas, and the ability to apply mathematical concepts and skills (for example, with regard to number, shape, pattern and measures). **Creative development** refers to the child's capacity to represent experiences of the world in a variety of ways and to respond to what can be seen, felt or heard. This can take a range of forms of expression, from imaginative play to drawing, painting, model-making, dance, drama, talk, music and interest in the creative work of others. Only some of this range can be examined here. **Knowledge and understanding of the world** refers to a child's development in finding out about the world – in particular, here, in relation to living things, materials and physical processes, energy, forces and how things function. It is about the growing ability to observe, predict, test, hypothesise, record findings and draw conclusions, communicate ideas and plan, make and evaluate designs.

The children

Four children have been chosen whose learning styles and personalities are quite different. This means that their routes to learning and the implications for teaching may also be quite different.

A brief description of each child, highlighting in particular her/his social and emotional development, will help to give a picture of the whole child.

Safaa

Safaa started in the nursery at 3 years 3 months. She is bilingual, and although she was familiar with some English when she started at school, Arabic is the language used at home. Her knowledge of English she had picked up from her older brother and sister and from television. Her parents are also fluent in English. At home she spends her time playing alone or with her brother and sister, and particularly enjoys playing imaginatively. She also enjoys helping her mother to cook and other similar activities.

She settled quite easily into the nursery, helped by her mother staying with her for most of each session during her first week. She was more at ease playing near a member of staff at first, and the home corner became a favourite place to play. On the few occasions when she was reluctant to let her mother leave her, playing 'families' and talking about her own family helped to settle her.

By the end of her first term in the nursery, Safaa had made a close friendship with one other girl, and the two would be frequently seen together. She was also happy to play in small groups of children, and did not like to be on her own in any activity. She was confident in relating to all members of staff.

She settled with ease into her reception class and soon made a group of new friends.

Faisal

Faisal also started nursery at 3 years and 3 months. His first language is Bengali, and he began at nursery with no previous experience of English. He settled into nursery easily and with confidence. At nursery he preferred to play alone, rather than with other children, whom he might join for very short periods. Because of this, many of the activities which staff planned for him encouraged him to become involved in small-group activities or to pair up with another child. Towards the end of his time in the nursery he was much more likely to sustain activities with others for longer periods of time, and occasionally would invite another child to play with him.

He settled quite well into the reception class, but found it difficult at first to settle to some of the teacher-initiated tasks, particularly in larger group situations. Towards the end of his first term he was finding this easier and was beginning to form a relationship with one other child.

Nicola

Nicola began in the nursery at 3 years 4 months. After seeming to settle in well at first, she became unsure about letting her mother leave her and needed to be near a member of staff, who would read to her to settle her. She was happy to become involved in small groups of other children of the same age (the children who started at the same time as her) so long as a member of staff was involved, and would often take quite a leading role in decisions about the play that ensued.

After her first term and a half her confidence about being at nursery began to grow. Nicola became much more independent of staff, and began to initiate play with several other children, going to find them and asking them to play with her. When involved in teacher-initiated activities she would ask who else would be joining the group. She initiated her own activities decisively, and then would come back to report to a member of staff what she had been doing. By the end of her time in the nursery, she enjoyed taking on the role of helping to settle and look after new children.

Nicola settled well into her new school, after the first half term of being quite shy with other children and staff she knew less well. She then began to take a leading role in some of the small-group activities she was involved with. After her first half term she became much more confident in the playground, leaving staff to go and play with a small group of friends.

James

James also began in the nursery at 3 years 3 months. He settled well into the nursery, but tended to shy away from staff at first. His parents had talked about his great interest in some of the popular cartoons on television and how he often talked about the characters from these. He quickly became involved in active play with a group of similar aged boys. Usually he played with children who shared a common interest in active imaginative play. During his time at the nursery he became increasingly at ease with the staff and other adults, and in joining in activities that the staff suggested he could try. After his first three terms (of five terms in nursery), James would enjoy staff becoming involved in his play, and was much more enthusiastic about involving himself in a range of activities he had not previously tried.

He settled well into the reception class, and enjoyed taking a leading role in activities as well as imaginative play with other children – boys and girls.

The starting point for knowing about any child's development when they enter a nursery or reception class is information about the child gathered from parents and carers. The stages of development highlighted here for each child were informed by what parents had said about their child at home, alongside observations made in their nursery and reception classes.

Language: Speaking & listening

James

FROM **3 years 3 months**

James uses short, simple phrases to ask questions, make requests and involve others in his play. Usually present tense, initiates talk to children but responds rather than initiates to staff. Pronunciation of some words a little unclear.

Implications for teaching
Staff to get involved with James by playing alongside him to help gain confidence in staff presence. Whilst doing so, talk about own actions and equipment being used, thereby modelling language, giving appropriate vocabulary and sentence structure.

Social skills Uses some talk to involve other children, and assign roles. Does not initiate contact with adults at nursery.

Attitude development Confident to address children but not staff.

Process skills Conveys simple messages, using some talk along with a lot of action to move play forward, able to express needs and wishes.

TO **4 years 4 months**

Came to tell his teacher today: 'Daddy and Mummy buyed me some new (super hero) toys. I keep getting more of them. I got this many now (shows fingers). Stephen got some too.' When showing another child how to play a role in an imaginative game he has initiated, he uses more actions than words. He is able to use talk to make up a story in his imaginative play.

Implications for teaching
Continue to encourage James to talk about events and interests beyond here and now of nursery life. Staff to become involved in his imaginative play, allowing him to take lead, encouraging him to use words to describe the actions and story of play.

Social skills Initiating talk to staff about himself and his friend; able to maintain play and inform larger groups of children and staff about his own imaginative play or real events. Confident to take lead with group of children.

Attitude development Confident to initiate conversations with known adults and children in a range of situations. Independent in choices of topics to talk about.

Process skills Able to use sentence structures which are more complex than before, covering a wider range of topics and purposes for talk. Still uses actions rather than words in giving instructions, but will attempt descriptions through words if asked to. Able to tell a story to others.

TO　　　　　　　　　　　　　　　　　　　　　　　　*5 years 6 months*

James described to a group of children how to play a new maths game, explained purpose and rules, and organised the turn-taking. Began by saying 'I know it, I'll show you what to do.' Uses a range of tenses in his talk correctly.

Implications for teaching
Continue to provide James with situations where he can take the lead in organising an activity and needs to describe what to do; encourage him to talk in small-group discussions on a range of subjects, to express his thoughts in discussions about possibilities and predictions.

Social skills Through talk, able to organise a group of children, almost without adult support.

Attitude development Independent in organising own time and activity. Keen to show/teach others what he knows.

Process skills Using some gesture, is able to give simple explanations which others could follow. Also able to describe purpose of activity. Uses past and future tenses, particularly in storytelling (past) and giving information about predicted events (future).

Concepts Understands that a particular sequence of events is necessary in a game.

Language: Speaking & listening

Faisal

FROM　　　　　　　　　　　　　　　　　　　　　　　*3 years 3 months*

English is a new language to Faisal. As he plays in the nursery he often talks to staff (in Bengali) to inform, ask questions and express his needs. Unfortunately, no staff member speaks Bengali. He also talks to accompany his play and actions. He is able to understand staff when gesture and visual clues are used to support the words.

Implications for teaching
Staff respond appropriately in English, talking about his play, using gesture and visual clues to accompany words. Use simple and clear statements.

TO　　　　　　　　　　　　　　　　　　　　　　　　*3 years 5 months*

Faisal named some fruit in a fruit bowl in English and some in Bengali. When given the name in English, he repeated it; also repeats some words if staff use simple sentences to accompany actions.

Implications for teaching
Continue to accompany words with visual clues and gestures, giving vocabulary appropriate to the situation.

Social skills Faisal likes to be near a member of staff, and talks happily in Bengali or shares the English he has learnt. Plays alongside other children.

Attitude development Faisal is confident to communicate in all the ways he can (mainly Bengali at present) with adults. Not confident to speak to other children.

Process skills Learning to speak new language, able to use words he knows in correct context, and to repeat new words and short phrases; able to make full use of gesture and visual clues to make his needs and wishes known and to understand.

TO	4 years 6 months

Faisal's English is now quite fluent and he is using full sentences – if unsure of a word he will say 'this one'. On an outing to the pet shop, Faisal talked in English almost continuously about his knowledge of the area, the cars we passed, his cousin's pet and how it got lost. He talked mainly to the member of staff, but occasionally spoke to another child, especially about the cars.

Implications for teaching
Continue to provide paired activities, encourage talk directly to other children rather than to staff. Continue to provide situations where he can talk about events from home life and his interests, to other children and staff. Encourage him to use Bengali with other Bengali-speaking children.

Social skills Very confident with adults, and increasingly confident at speaking to other children. Also listens well to their comments too. Prefers to be with adult or very small group of children and adult.

Attitude development Confident in expressing himself in English over a wide range of topics. Happy to be given new vocabulary.

Process skills Nearly fluent in a second language now, able to use correct sentence structure, although verb endings not always correct. If given new word, will usually try to use it. Able to give information (expressing his knowledge), to tell story (about cousin's pet), and to join in discussion with others.

TO	5 years 3 months

In the more formal school settings Faisal speaks quietly and needs to be invited to contribute. Use of tenses not always correct, but has a wide vocabulary. In less formal settings with staff involvement, such as swimming and outings, he will volunteer

information and talk more readily. With his peers he is more communicative and will use a louder voice. On the recent outing to a farm, Faisal talked at length and excitedly about the animals, sharing his knowledge with peers and adults.

Implications for teaching
Continue to provide situations where Faisal will feel at ease and able to contribute to discussion – e.g. small groups, more informal discussions where teacher involved as group member.

Social skills It took Faisal some time to settle into primary school, and he is still gaining confidence in talking to staff openly in the same way that he communicates with his peers. In less formal school settings, much more confident.

Attitude development Able to volunteer information and his knowledge in certain situations, and to give his reasons, particularly in areas which interest him (e.g. science activities).

Process skills Able to explain what he has done in an activity or task, and to demonstrate his understanding through language (e.g. in maths or science). Able to tell storyline to friends and share information and express his reasoning in less formal settings.

Language: Writing

Safaa

FROM	3 years 3 months

During her imaginative play, wrote two messages and put them in envelopes – on first, drew lines then made marks in different pen and named them 'abc'; the second was a letter for her sister, again made up of lines.

Implications for teaching
Continue to provide writing materials in lots of areas such as home corner, provide models for writing and displays, such as alphabet displays – when occasions arise, point these out to Safaa. Encourage writing in her play to continue. Write name with her on her work, and ask her if she would like something else to be written too.

Social skills Group role play is the context for her writing; purpose of her writing is to communicate with family members.

Attitude development Independently chose to write; second letter written on encouragement by staff member. Proud of her achievement.

Process skills Makes individual marks for writing, different from her drawing marks. Knows names of some letters and knows that letters are written down.

Concepts Understands purpose for writing – a letter – but not yet putting content into it. Understands writing is made up of letters

Physical development Correct grip on graphic tools; uses a variety of movements making straight lines and circular patterns.

TO   *4 years 3 months*

Safaa continues to write in her role play, but has increased her range of purposes – shopping lists, notices and letters. She incorporates the letters she knows into her own writing (s, o). In this sample – a shopping list – Safaa said 'It says coca cola, fresh cheese.'

Implications for teaching
On some occasions write words with her (e.g. make own shopping list), showing her how these words are written. Help her to recognise and write her own name.

TO   *4 years 5 months*

Safaa wrote her whole name today for first time, asking staff member for confirmation as she wrote each letter. Used capitals to do it: no models available of her name in capitals in the nursery, so doing it from memory of what she does at home.

Implications for teaching
Congratulate her on achievement. On some occasions, point out differences between upper and lower case letters. Draw her attention to initial letter sounds and shapes of other letters.

Social skills Group role play still forms major context for her writing. Able to show independence – wrote name on leaflet so she didn't lose it.

Attitude development Independent and confident to use writing in different situations for different purposes. In second example, Safaa felt great sense of achievement in what she had done.

Process skills Able to incorporate her skills in letter formation into purposeful writing. Able to write letters of own name from memory in correct sequence, named them correctly.

Concepts Understands that there is a common code for writing, and that letters are used in different combinations to write messages, or names. Understands writing conveys a meaning.

Physical development Increasing hand control in letter formation.

TO   *5 years 6 months*

Continues to incorporate writing into her role play, now using what she knows about combining letters, initial letter sounds, and consonant sounds. Depending on purpose of writing, will write using these or, if a telephone message, will write using own emergent writing squiggles representing joined up writing.

Implications for teaching
Continue to reinforce and build up phonic knowledge; when writing in set tasks and in play continue to encourage her to try out spelling for herself. Make sure she knows how to write all the letters of alphabet and knows how each letter sounds. Build on social purposes for writing – e.g. situations where she is writing genuine messages to others.

Social skills Uses writing to communicate messages to other children and adults (in notices in classroom). Most of her reasons for writing are social.

Attitude development Confident in her use of writing, and in her own ability to form words and convey meaning.

Process skills Able to make connection between word and sound, and to use this in her writing. Building up a memory of words she can write and spell.

Concepts Understands connection in English between speech sound and written form; knows correct print direction; and that each letter has two forms (capital and lower case).

Language: Writing

Faisal

FROM   *3 years 5 months*

Faisal writes his own name on drawings and models as a zigzag line, in either direction horizontally. If staff write his name for him on his painting, he paints over this carefully before he paints anything else. Very interested in letters on computer keyboard and can find letter F.

Implications for teaching
Build on interest in computer keyboard and alphabet, give him access to word processing program on computer. Look at alphabet books with him; staff to model writing for him – i.e. write own writing alongside him and talk about what you are writing.

Attitude development Confident in writing his own name in his emergent writing.

Process skills Makes writing-like marks quite distinct from drawing; recognises first letter of own name in English.

Concepts Understands writing is different from other mark-making. Knows names can be written down. Knows letter F.

Physical development Correct grip on pen, right-handed.

TO

'Dad walking to his work.'

Can write his name in English and Bengali (emergent Bengali writing). Interested in writing letters, e.g. a letter to his Dad and another one to Father Christmas; made book himself with paper, hole puncher and tags, then said he didn't know what to do. Teacher suggested he drew pictures first – he drew his family doing different things. When teacher suggested he wrote about the pictures or wrote the story, he said 'I can't write, you do it!' Persuaded him to try and showed him a sample of what he had done before, he then confidently wrote on every page, using his own emergent writing, and copying the name of another child.

'It's Chantal.'

TO

Able to write several names from memory – favourite is 'BMW' which he knows from the car! Daily practises his newly acquired skills.

Implications for teaching
Continue to make books with him, suggest a topic for him, e.g. one of his interests – pets, cars, etc. Continue to encourage him to try for himself and help him make phonic connections with initial letters of words. Help him to increase his word bank.

Faisal copied this word from a book cover

Social skills Confident in small group, but prefers to have staff nearby.

Attitude development With staff encouragement can gain enough confidence to try out new things for himself using his existing skills and knowledge. Motivated to practise his newly acquired skills: shows determination and persistence.

Process skills Able to apply what he knows (e.g. print direction, letter formation, combining different letters to write new words) to new situation and context. Increasing number of words written from memory (names mostly).

Concepts Knows that words are written in a particular way; knows words can be copied or he can try for himself.

Faisal is enjoying using the writing area, and often chooses to write here, to take his writing home or to give it to staff member as a 'present'. In this writing he uses all his knowledge of letters, and puts them in different combinations on the page. If asked to read this writing he laughs. In all his writing he writes from left to right across the page, and can now write from memory all letters of the alphabet, several names and several words. Will copy words to write own sentence.

Implications for teaching
Continue to support him in same way, building up his word bank and phonic knowledge. Give him audiences to write for. Talk to him about his 'play' writing, possibly read back some of it to him, encouraging him to make phonic connections. Help him particularly with vowel sounds.

Social skills Social purpose to much of his writing now; writes frequently independently without being asked to. Much more confident with staff.

Attitude development Confident to use what he knows to make up own writing; also confident to ask for model to be given to him.

Process skills Can write in clear letter formation all letters of alphabet. Writes own and brother's name. Correct print direction. Able to copy words correctly to make a sentence.

Concepts Aware his own writing of words cannot be read as proper words.

Language: Reading

James

James enjoys listening to short stories read to him and has definite favourites which he asks for. Looks at pictures closely and names objects he recognises, sometimes using simple sentence structure.

Implications for teaching
Continue to read and look at favourite books with him as often as possible. Introduce some new stories and story props for him to develop knowledge of storyline.

Social skills Confident to request favourite stories when staff suggest reading to him, happy to listen in group or alone. This is a situation in which James feels more at ease with staff.

Attitude development Interested in books and pictures in books.

Process skills Uses pictures to name characters and objects. Listens attentively to favourite known texts and other short stories in picture books.

TO   *4 years 6 months*

Teacher reading to small group of children asked James where she should begin. James pointed to words and ran finger along first line of print, right to left on first page and left to right on next. When asked if he would like to read, James retold story from pictures in known book and from memory of text to staff member and two other children, then asked to take it home.

Implications for teaching
Continue to read in small-group situations to James, increasing his knowledge of a wider range of stories. Continue to ask him to retell stories to small group. Point out other features of print to him.

Social skills Confident to retell story from book to staff and children in small group.

Attitude development Confident to demonstrate his knowledge of books to others.

Process skills Uses memory of text and knowledge of book language to retell story from book; focuses on pictures rather than words but knows it is words which are read. Not yet sure of correct direction of print in English.

Concepts Developing understanding of some of the conventions relating to print and reading process – e.g. that print tells the story.

TO   *5 years 8 months*

James can read several words independently, recognises names of most of the children in the class, and enjoys picking out words he knows in the displays around the class. He is able to work out unknown words in simple texts from picture and context cues, with some help from initial letter sounds. Enjoys looking at books with his peers, and will retell stories, mostly relying on his memory.

Implications for teaching
Continue to build up his knowledge of words from memory and phonic knowledge, beginning with initial sounds. Help him guess from grapho-phonic cues.

Social skills Sees reading as a social event, but also reads alone.

Attitude development Confident to use all his available strategies when reading in a one-to-one or small-group situation.

Process skills Able to use initial letter sound of word, context, memory and sight vocabulary, and picture cues.

Language: Reading

Nicola

FROM	3 years 4 months

Nicola enjoys having stories read to her and has definite favourites which she chooses to take home. Always joins in with any repeating lines and phrases, and anticipates what might happen next from pictures. Retells familiar stories using story props (cut-out pictures of characters in story). Sometimes will relate picture in book to her own personal experience: 'I got one like that.'

Implications for teaching
Continue to provide story props for an increasing number of stories, and once she knows story, suggest she retells to another child. Continue to provide stories with repeating lines for Nicola to join in. Allow her plenty of time to talk about story/pictures when reading with her.

Social skills Sees reading as a social activity. Will retell story to other children if staff member is available.

Attitude development Enjoys all that stories offer. Confident to use her skills in storytelling with a small group. Listens attentively and initiates discussion with staff about book.

Process skills Uses memory to join in with repeating lines; uses picture and semantic cues to predict what might happen. Uses memory to retell familiar stories. Uses picture cues to talk about book.

Concepts Knows it is possible to predict from pictures and meaning; knows story can be retold without the book; knows it is possible to relate own life experiences to a story book.

TO	4 years 6 months

Recognises name in writing.
Knows many stories off by heart, and will use book as a prompt to retelling these or can retell without. Retold three stories at story time to small group of children, using lots of intonation. Read a story to her teacher, recalling 60 per cent of text and making up rest from picture cues. Often heard using 'book language' in her play (e.g. 'and there was a mighty splash' and 'he drank all the water in the tap'). Enjoys making up rhyming words (e.g. 'doggie poggie') and will sound out initial letter ('der...dee, per...pee'). Recognises many letters of the alphabet. Enjoys making own books from well-known stories, asking staff to scribe.

Implications for teaching
Continue in same way, asking her to read to others, and build on her phonic initial letter knowledge; help her to relate her knowledge of writing with reading, asking her to try to guess at initial letter of words when scribing for her.

Social skills Confident to retell story to group with or without staff present. Confident to take lead with younger children.

Attitude development Continues to enjoy what books and stories offer. Enjoys using her skills and knowledge and sharing these.

Process skills Recognises some letters, identifies some letter sounds, uses memory for retelling known stories and picture cues for others; incorporates what she has learnt from stories into other activities and own storytelling.

Concepts Makes link between some letters and sound. Knows stories are written down by people and that she can do this too.

TO   *5 years 6 months*

Nicola has a well developed bank of words she can read from memory and is well on the way to fluency, reading increasingly complex texts and using a variety of cues to tackle unknown words. If unsure, will try and work it out before asking.
Her interest in stories and books continues and she enjoys discussing stories with peers and staff. Able to create own word patterns in writing as well as speech (e.g. cat, mat).
Knows all letters and sounds of the alphabet. Enjoys acting out a story in small group of friends, but prefers not to take leading role. Enjoys sitting in book area with friends reading to self and others and discussing the stories.

Implications for teaching
Continue to provide wide range of opportunities to read and build on phonic and graphic knowledge. Introduce her to information books and encourage her to use by setting up paired/small-group discussions on these.

Social skills Social confidence continues and sees books as something to be shared. Confident at reading to staff in small group or individual situation.

Attitude development Books and reading continue to be important to Nicola; often chooses to read independently when finished other set tasks. Confident in own growing ability to read, and tries for herself before asking for help.

Process skills Able to use phonic (initial letter and known combinations), picture and context cues to guess at unknown words. Relies on her memory too. Able to use set patterns of letter combinations to make words up. Able to evaluate stories.

Concepts Knows all letter sounds and several regular patterns, knows how stories are made (beginning, middle, end, as well as more complex structures). Knows reading requires a combination of skills and strategies, and is able to use these.

Creative development

James

James is very interested in playing firefighters (based on his knowledge of a popular cartoon) and plays this daily with one or two others. Does not choose to use pens and paper independently and very unsure how to hold pens. Today, when encouraged to draw he drew this (see sample) and said 'It's a fire engine.' Did this quickly, then called to others who were also drawing: 'Ring, ring! It's the fire engine!' Ran back to climbing frame.

Implications for teaching
Continue to provide tools and occasions for drawing in his imaginative play, and encourage to try. Develop knowledge around his interests (e.g. firefighting procedures). Introduce him to a broad range of creative activities.

Social skills Plays in small group with others who have similar interests; responds to staff if staff initiate contact.

Attitude development Confident in acting out a role he has knowledge of; cautious in new situations where he feels less sure of what to do. Chooses familiar activities and repeats these.

Physical development Good control when running, pushing, pulling carts, cautious when climbing; loose fist grip on pen half-way up.

Process skills Able to act out a simple storyline involving plenty of physical action. Drawing: uses small range of mainly circular movements with pen, represents on paper what he plays physically.

Concepts Understands it is possible to represent play experiences or objects on paper; understands some of process of firefighting.

TO	4 years 2 months

James continues to spend time acting out roles from cartoon or television programmes with a group of others, and takes the lead in initiating this. He has just begun to choose to draw for himself, and will do several drawings at a time. Also paints often. He has begun to draw human representations, usually one of each member of his family, mostly using same format; occasionally these will be figures from his 'super hero' play. He has also begun to make 3D 'props' for his role play, on encouragement from another child, who usually helps him with cutting out. Storyline in role play is more fully developed, and is beginning to be able to tell the story to others who are not involved.

Implications for teaching
Continue to encourage him to participate in a wide range of 2D and 3D creative activities, helping him to build up physical fine-motor control. Continue to ask him to tell others the storyline in play and begin to introduce idea of telling own stories to small group at story time, starting with making up a joint story amongst a group of his friends.

Social skills Takes a leading role in role-play activities, initiating the story and physical actions required; confident in group situation. Initiates contact with staff as well as responds.

Attitude development Organises own time, participates in a wide range of activities out of choice, including those previously felt very tentative about. Beginning to reflect on own learning – e.g. talks about new achievements. Happy to try out something new.

Physical development Firmer control on pens/pencils, correct grip, right-hand; beginning to hold scissors correctly, but needs help to cut *out* rather than *up!* Confident in climbing and jumping.

Process skills Finds own materials appropriate to task or will ask if unsure. Uses a limited range of formats in his 2D representations. Makes representations of objects/artefacts for a purpose: to use in play. Able to tell simple story of his play in words as well as actions.

Concepts Understands an increasing range of techniques and ways of representing (3D, 2D, drama). Understands a story can be told as well as acted out.

TO	5 years 4 months

Drew a picture of 'super heroes' including detail of facial features, limbs, hands, using 'correct' colours to represent them; very carefully coloured in; included insignia on their clothes, and their 'props' (e.g. weapons, pets, etc). Made model of scene from cartoon film with group of three others – James took lead in initiating this. When asked how he knew what to do, he said 'Well, I've got this book about it at home.'
Regularly helps younger children to make costumes and 3D objects or will do it for them. Will dictate storyline of role play to staff to make books which he illustrates, and includes own writing.

Implications for teaching
Encourage him to continue to use his skills to help younger children. Increase range of models and props he can make beyond cartoon characters – e.g. help with props for assemblies, illustrating class-made books.

Social skills Takes lead with other children, welcoming new children to join in a joint activity. Confident to work alone; confident with staff.

Attitude development Independent in choice of activity and chooses broad range. Able to carry out idea in a group on request of teacher, with a little teacher support, and to sustain this.

Physical development Fine motor control well established in cutting, drawing, modelling

Process skills Uses a range of 'formulas' now to represent different things, and combines these to fit purpose. Includes a lot of detail in 3D plasticine modelling representations. Able to dictate story in narrative form.

Concepts Understands wide range of ways of representing objects, scenes and experiences.

Creative development

Safaa

FROM   *3 years 6 months*

Becomes very involved in role play to do with homes and families, and often dresses up. She paints and draws when invited to by staff, but rarely without a prompt. **Painting:** *makes blobs and squiggles, using all available colours, or blocks of colours interlocking if using smaller equipment.* **Drawings:** *small separate marks more like writing marks. Does not name or discuss either paintings or drawings.* **Dance:** *very keen to join in dance sessions, and enjoys representing animals/insects as well as responding to music through her movements.*

Implications for teaching
Continue to offer a breadth of provision and invite her to it, draw her attention to colours and name them for her, develop interest in mixing colours; give her a commentary as she paints or draws, pointing out the colours, shapes and patterns she is making. Observe role play further with a view to helping her develop the stories.

Social skills Confident in small-group situations. Prefers to join in any activity with her friend.

Attitude development Needs encouragement from staff to join in full range of activities (e.g. to be motivated to involve herself in 2D or 3D activities); very independent in role play, drama and dance.

Process skills Able to act out a range of roles in home-type role play, and adds to storyline initiated by others; able to use a range of techniques in painting for making different marks; in drawing, makes small individual marks; in dance, uses a range of movements for different purposes.

Concepts Mark-making but not overtly symbolic representation, understands possibility of representing through dance and drama.

Physical development Good control of large muscle movements, correct grip on pen.

TO   *4 years 6 months*

Building towers (calls them castles) with blocks, precariously balanced, but seems most interested in height of tower; paints and draws out of choice, often enclosing shapes, some representational drawing on request (e.g. ladders for snakes and ladders game) but otherwise rarely discusses her drawings or paintings.

Continues to enjoy house-type role play, and this has become more complex, involving going on holiday, swimming and visits to hospital. Will assign a role by explaining game to another child who wants to join in, and today asked two adult visitors if they would play, explaining the game to them in detail and introducing other children.

Implications for teaching

Continue to encourage more building and construction activities, offering support and extending her experience here. Talk more frequently to her about her drawings. Begin to suggest that some of her stories in role play could be made into story books to share with others, staff to scribe.

Safaa's ladders

Social skills Helps others to join in with her play, welcomes staff or children; prefers to be with chosen friends than involved in something alone. Confident to involve others she doesn't know in her play.

Attitude development Increasingly independent in use of time across the broad range of curricular provision, but prefers to do this with friends; growing in confidence in choosing something new.

Process skills Able to tell storyline of her play to others and to use talk and imagination to develop and sustain play; wider range of techniques and marks used in painting and drawing – enclosed shapes, grids, straight lines.

Concepts Beginning to represent using 2D and 3D materials and techniques (e.g. drawing and building).

TO   *5 years 7 months*

Asked her teacher to write down one of her stories and wanted to act it out in front of others with her friends, but when it came to doing it became quite shy and asked her friend to take leading role.
Construction: After looking at book about 'Sleeping Beauty', created a castle out of large construction set with a friend, making enough space for them both to sit in – friend suggested they enlarge it as not quite big enough at first. Then, on encouragement from teacher, decorated walls with drawings of kings, queens, etc. Asked to pick flowers in school garden to put inside. Put sign on door with name of castle on it.

Implications for teaching

Continue to provide her with more traditional tales from a range of cultures as inspiration for her. Continue scribing her stories and ask her to illustrate them. Encourage her to act in front of small group of friends. Introduce building with other construction sets and modelling with clay and plasticine.

Social skills Friends are very important to her: likes and wants to be part of a group; gaining in confidence in front of audience, but still shy at present. Relates with confidence to all staff.

Attitude development Decisive and independent now at initiating own creative task as long as can work with another child. Confident in trying something new. Persistent with task until completed to her satisfaction.

Process skills Able to dictate story with beginning, middle and end using 'story language'. Able to create a hollow cuboid with construction set. Drawings include increasing details – full facial features, coloured-in clothes, limbs.

Physical development Good control of drawing tools and scissors, manages to screw up bolts and nuts quite tight.

Concepts Able to apply knowledge of 3D shapes, and stories.

Knowledge & understanding of the world
(particularly aspects of science and technology)

Nicola

FROM	3 years 4 months

Technology: Explores materials in craft and technology workshop area – tries out scissors, glue, tape, string, sewing; examines and uses different papers and cardboard boxes.
Science: Joined in with a group of children and teacher blowing different objects across water, saying to teacher 'look it's gone down' when a boat sank. Then took straw and blew bubbles in water; talked about trying to blow 'bigger bubbles'.

Implications for teaching
Continue to encourage Nicola's explorations of equipment around the nursery, showing her the possibilities with the range of equipment. Involve her in other science investigations with air and water, as well as flotation.

Social skills Confident to join in with small group if staff member there.

Attitude development Chooses and explores materials and their properties independently. Talks about her intentions, and persistent in trying to achieve these.

Process skills Able to use a range of fixing materials appropriately, including sewing (once shown how). Able to talk about her observations and intentions.

Physical development Holds scissors well and can use to cut up paper with good control; able to sew large stitches.

Science: Nicola shows a wide range of interests both in materials and the natural environment – e.g. in observing insects and plants, and experimenting with magnets, mirrors, water, sand. Involved in experiment dissolving different substances in water. Very careful and methodical in carrying out instructions – e.g. two pipettes of water in each dish of powder/substance. Counted out loud and encouraged her friend to do the same. Talked about what she saw: 'Look it's all gone, I can't see it' (salt); 'it's the same' (sand); 'it's like porridge' (flour).

Implications for teaching

Invite her to take a leading role in other similar experiments with dissolving, choosing different substances. Take photos and make book of the investigation with her as a resource for the class, including her predictions and comments. Continue to encourage her questioning approach.

Social skills Independent of staff in choice of activity; will join in small group without staff member present.

Attitude development Confident in expressing her observations. Chooses own materials independently; confident and organised in carrying out instructions.

Process skills Able to follow a sequence of actions; able to organise own materials; able to talk about her observations.

Concepts Understands that adding water may change a substance or may not. Understands that living plants and creatures need certain conditions to survive.

Science: Nicola independently made an electric circuit with a motor. First shown how to do this five months earlier, but not since. Knew where to find equipment and sorted correct pieces required. When teacher suggested adding a switch to circuit, joined circuit adding switch but omitting battery. Tried switch but no result; teacher suggested something might be wrong: Nicola realised battery was not connected and held up battery and laughed. With help, reconnected whole circuit. Afterwards put everything away in correct place.

Implications for teaching

Build on knowledge and skills related to electric circuits, giving her questions to investigate. Encourage working in pairs. Can she think of ways to *record* her investigations (e.g. drawings, writing)?

Attitude development Independent in performing task of own choice; once established that there was a problem, hypothesised cause.

Process skills Able to remember a process she had been shown and could repeat. Able to choose own materials and put them away.

Concepts Understands that battery makes something happen in electric circuit (bulb to light up, motor to spin) and that there is a correct way to join up a circuit.

Knowledge & understanding of the world
(particularly aspects of science and technology)

Faisal

FROM	3 years 5 months

Technology: In craft and technology workshop area, watched another child sewing, nodded when staff member asked him if he wanted a turn, found straws and buttons and sewed these onto material, accompanying his actions with noises 'weee' as pulled thread tight.

Science: In making electric circuit, chose right equipment, but needed help to join up circuit correctly; became very interested in buzzers, first one kind, then another, then indicated he wanted to use both at same time. Listened to noises with great concentration.

Implications for teaching
Encourage and involve him in a wide range of activities in the workshop, making sure he can understand with ease. Build on his interest in circuits, possibly adding circuits to a construction model, e.g. a large wheeled construction with a buzzer. Use a buzzer as front door bell to dolls house or home corner, show him how to add switch to circuit.

Social skills Observes other children, then chooses what he finds interesting; confident with all staff; likes to be near member of staff or alone. Asks staff for help when he wants it (in first language).

Attitude development Confident to indicate choices; persistent in what he has chosen to do. Explores materials systematically.

Process skills Chooses own materials independently.

Physical development Able to sew through small-holed material and thread small items on to a needle.

TO	4 years 6 months

Science: Spent nearly all morning making circuits with motors today; helped other children join up their circuits and showed them what he was doing. Cut out circle of paper and placed on top of motor, held pen on paper, stopped motor and looked at pattern; on suggestion from staff, tried other shapes of paper, tried drawing a picture, then put on motor and watched effect.

Implications for teaching
Provide paired activities as far as possible. Show him different ways small motors can be used; make spinning tops using match sticks and card; encourage him to colour with different patterns. Ask him to show others what he has done.

TO *4 years 10 months*

Science: Watched others making and flying paper 'helicopters'. Then made his own. Tried holding it in several different ways to see which flew best, then added more paper clips; finally made one very small and one large, held one in each hand, predicted which would land first, then let go.

Implications for teaching

Continue to extend range of knowledge and possible activities, feeding his interest in investigating.

Social skills Faisal mainly gets involved in activities on his own or in parallel with others, but enjoys helping them. Very confident with staff.

Attitude development On occasional suggestion from staff, can independently set up own tests and experiments; persists until he feels he has achieved his intention.

Process skills Able to follow procedure required to make many things, from electric circuits to parachutes; systematic in way he sets up a test, able to make verbal predictions; once this has been modelled for him by staff he will encourage others to do it.

Concepts Has some understanding of idea of setting up a fair test, and will sometimes follow this, usually in order to produce most dramatic effect. Developing concepts over range of content.

TO *5 years 6 months*

Science: Goes immediately to any science activity or equipment put out, including natural science. Faisal became very involved in observing eggs hatching, tadpoles developing and growing seeds. Recorded what he saw by drawing a sequence of development with tadpoles, and, although he missed out one stage, he realised what he had done and was able to talk about the complete life cycle. Experiments with magnets, sorting what was attracted to magnets, from other items; also recorded this by drawing.

Implications for teaching

Continue to offer a broad range of provision for scientific investigations. Ask him to predict what might happen and give his reasons. Help him to record these (e.g. by making books, or making displays with others).

Attitude development Faisal is confident to explore materials, and experiment independently, and continues to show persistence. Shares what he knows about growth, as well as what he sees.

Process skills Able to record his observations through drawing.

Concepts Understands the sequence of growth and development in some species of living things.
Understands magnets will attract some types of materials and not others.

Mathematics

Nicola

FROM	3 years 3 months

In home corner, matched six spoons to six plates and said 'They're all coming – 123584.'
Made shapes with finger in dry sand, said 'I done a circle... I done a square.....I done a dot.'
While having a story read to her, Nicola talked about sequence of day: 'It's getting dark. I'll have dinner when I get home, then I go to bed. I have breakfast when I get up.'
In building with blocks, realised she needed a 'square' to fill up a gap in a pattern she'd made from 'squares' and 'rectangles'.

Implications for teaching
Model correct counting for her when occasion arises. Build on interest and awareness of shape and pattern – provide shape 'hunts' around nursery in small group. Introduce more stories and discussions about time, and build on this in role-play situations.

Social skills Applies mathematical knowledge and concepts in her play with staff member and two children. Confident in explaining to adult what she has done.

Attitude development Independently using her already acquired mathematical knowledge, skills and concepts. Able to talk about these in her play, and expresses sense of achievement.

Process skills In block play, beginning to apply knowledge to solve problems, and discuss this. Able to describe sequence of day using personal examples. Matches up to six items; counts correctly to 3.

Concepts Although numerals not in correct sequence, understands purpose of numerals with small numbers. *Time:* understands sequence of day by events. Identifies 2D shapes and can differentiate these.

TO	4 years 2 months

Initiated with another child sorting all model animals by families, regardless of make of model.
On finding three teddy bears, re-enacted Three Bears story by finding three different sized chairs, bowls, spoons and made graded beds out of blocks.
Uses sorting toys to make up own stories, and sorts by a range of different attributes, often two simultaneously.

Looking at number book, recognises numerals 1 – 10, and can count accurately.
Took a drinks chart around all the staff, asking who wanted tea/coffee. Filled it in independently after her teacher had modelled what to do. Put marks in chart correctly and able to read back information she had gathered.

Afternoon Drinks

Tea	| | /
Coffee	| |
Orange juice	|

Implications for teaching

Set up a variety of sorting challenges for her with a variety of materials and invite her to describe what she has done. Continue to provide reasons for making charts and gathering data – help her to make her own charts. Extend her knowledge of numbers.

Social skills Initiating maths-focused activities with one other child and with staff. Independently carried out a survey requesting information from staff.

Attitude development Independently collecting data. Shares knowledge.

Process skills Able to choose and find suitable materials independently; able to apply teacher's strategy for collecting data; able to set up own criteria for sorting; recognises numerals and can count to 10.

Concepts Understands there are different ways of sorting; understands data collected can be recorded and read. Able to order by size.

TO   *5 years 6 months*

Nicola recognises and can write numbers to at least 20. She is aware of number bonds to 5 and can do simple addition and subtraction up to 10. She is able to organise several maths games between herself and a partner, describing rules clearly in sequence. She recognises some coins and is able to pay correctly in the class shop with correct whole coins.
With a partner, she has made two bar charts with only a little help – one on travel to school and one on shoes worn by class members; explained this to her teacher.

Implications for teaching

Continue to build on skills and understandings with numbers to 20. Introduce more complex maths games for her, but also encourage her to share her knowledge of games with younger children. Build up skills in other areas – e.g. telling time; get her to record the information on charts in other ways and introduce new investigations.

Social skills Enjoys joint activities with a partner and joining in with larger groups (e.g. in shop). Confident to explain to staff what she has done.

Attitude development Confident in approach to mathematical tasks set by teacher and able to set up her own independently.

Process skills Able to organise own data collection, perform functions with low numbers, use correct coinage, and describe rules of game to friend.

Concepts Understanding of number is developing – concept of low numbers well established.

Mathematics

Faisal

FROM	3 years 3 months

Faisal lined up cars parallel to each other in rows, sorted out all the small cuboid blocks and lined them up similarly, talking in Bengali as he does this. Made a wall two rows high with milk cartons at milk table, later made a similar pattern with blocks.
Fitted cars on a flat board in rows covering all of surface; counted to 3 in English. When drawing, draws parallel horizontal lines on paper, usually doing several at one time.

Implications for teaching
Build on interest in parallel lines and lengths in lots of situations – e.g. rolling dough, collage, train set, large blocks outside. Draw his models to show him the patterns he makes. Continue interest in block play.

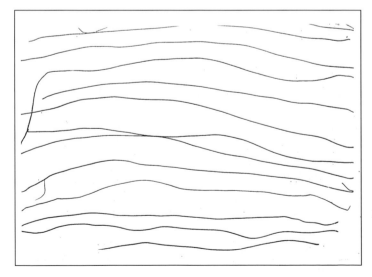

Social skills Involves himself in activities independently of other children and adults, but if adult also involved he will talk to them in Bengali, using lots of gesture and smiles.

Physical development Very precise in how he places objects, balancing and lining up in straight lines.

Attitude development Persistent in pursuing a set of ideas into many different activities, using a wide range of materials, solving problems independently as he explores properties of materials in this way.

Process skills Sorts by shape, uses objects to cover an area, explores properties of shapes, organises own materials.

Concepts Classifies objects according to attributes he is interested in. Understands objects in a set can be counted.

TO   *4 years 6 months*

Block play: replaces all blocks back into box, matching up longer blocks with correct number of shorter blocks, placing other shapes into symmetrical formations. Named 2D shapes and talked about how many edges each one had. Named shapes another child was making with blocks ('star, sun').
Counts to 12. Knows configuration of dots on dice and moves pieces in board games accurately. Made collage of 12 objects for number frieze and helped to display all numbers in correct order.
Independently set up investigation with toy car on road he had made with planks, marking how far he could get car to go with chalk; involved another child in this. Followed this by rolling tyres down slide.

Implications for teaching

Set him specific challenges in block play (e.g. length of blocks as long as carpet/room); invite him to make up own shapes and name them; introduce positional language; suggest other ideas to investigate in pair; build on knowledge of number.

Social skills Most activities and investigations carried out alone, but beginning to sustain play with others and involve them in his investigations without adult support.

Attitude development Very independent in pursuing own ideas, setting up investigations and problem-solving in his play.

Process skills Beginning to record his investigations after staff had modelled this for him. Applies his knowledge about shape, number and measurement to what he does.

Concepts Understanding of number up to 12 (that 12 refers to 12 objects); understands 2D shapes are defined by number of edges, and that shorter lengths are fractions of longer ones.

TO 5 years 3 months

Able to find 2D shapes on request, and identify them by number of sides. Able to choose correct 3D shapes by name and use these to make a model.
Can write all numerals to 10, and understands that 0 stands for nothing. Can add and subtract using objects under 10; under 6 can do this mentally.
Understands 'taller than' and 'shorter than' and can order in sequence a number of objects by length, although uses word 'small' or 'big' to describe them.

Implications for teaching

Introduce addition and subtraction, using numerals as well as objects. Support him in naming shapes, size and positional language; involve in more investigations in a pair.

Attitude development Able to carry out set task on request by adult, independently or with adult nearby.

Process skills Able to write numerals correctly to 10, add and subtract numbers of objects up to 10, and do this mentally up to 6; can order objects by length.

Concepts Increasing knowledge and understanding of properties of different shapes. Increasing understanding of number, including zero.

Teachers have a curriculum of knowledge, skills and attitudes that they wish to teach to all the children in their classes, whether based on an early years curriculum or the National Curriculum. Yet what has been highlighted in this chapter is the differences between children in the way that they learn, resulting from their different experiences and skills, and their different attitudes and approaches to learning. However, a common thread has emerged through the course of the chapter: **the importance of building on what interests and motivates the child**. For Safaa, role play was the meaningful context for her development in writing; for Faisal, block play was an important context for much of his mathematical development. But Faisal and Safaa will not be the only children in the class for whom these particular contexts are important.

In order that children are motivated and helped to fulfil their true potential in their education, teachers need to be able to respond effectively to their individual interests and learning patterns.

5 Some Common Questions Answered

This chapter answers some of the common questions asked by teachers who have begun to track significant achievement of children in nursery and reception classes.

▶ **How does the system recommended here for nursery and reception classes fit with what the rest of the teachers in the school will be doing?**

The approach to assessment used in this book is recommended as a way of assessing children which fits in very well with all the recent recommendations made by the QCA, DFEE and OFSTED in relation to early years education. Although the curriculum used in the early years is different from the National Curriculum, early years teachers will have highlighted children's significant achievements in similar, but broader, areas of learning to those of the National Curriculum. By the end of the reception year, these achievements will also relate to the expectations of the National Literacy and Numeracy Strategies for this age, as the learning objectives for the reception year will have been planned for. So, whether or not the school continues to use this approach in Key Stages 1 and 2, the information gathered and passed on will no doubt be useful.

However, many schools do find that this approach to assessment and recording can be usefully continued throughout the primary age range. This is because it encompasses a broad view of development, including the social, physical and attitude dimensions of learning, and teachers know that real significant achievement means more than children just meeting planned or prescribed learning intentions in each subject area. Such information gathered from examples of significant achievements can be used for children's Records of Achievements and for setting individual targets with children across the primary school, especially as they incorporate the element of *self*-assessment, crucial to target setting.

▶ **Does this system fulfil the requirements for assessment from bodies such as OFSTED or the DFEE or recommendations from the QCA?**

The Early Learning Goals are defined as goals that *'most children are expected to achieve by the end of the reception year'* (QCA, 1999). These are like 'end-of-Key Stage statements' for the Foundation Stage – which covers the learning for children from 3 to nearly 6 years. Although these do not form a statutory or legal requirement, all the official education bodies (the DFEE, QCA and OFSTED) are in agreement with them, and when OFSTED inspectors inspect nursery and reception classes they look to see how far the planning and teaching will lead children to achieve these goals in each area of learning. It is expected that the six areas of learning will be used for planning. In terms of assessment, the *Curriculum Guidance for the Foundation Stage* (QCA, 2000) gives advice on what should be the aim of assessment and the kinds of processes which should be used. For example, it advises that *'practitioners make systematic observations and assessments of each child's achievements, interests and learning styles'* and *'use these observations and assessments to identify learning priorities and plan relevant and motivating learning experiences...'*.

The QCA also talks about the importance of *'observations which are evaluated, recorded and shared regularly with parents'*. In Chapter 6 we look at how best to share records with parents from the beginning of their child's time with you.

As far as OFSTED is concerned, part of the requirements from OFSTED for assessment throughout the primary age range is that information gathered from assessment is used to inform future planning. Tracking significant achievement in the way outlined is designed to fulfil all the above requirements. Using the matrix shown in Chapter 1 will ensure tracking across the early years curriculum in different aspects of learning and thus provides a good system for monitoring learning. As each record is specific to each individual child, it is sure to provide vital evidence of whatever progress and development is taking place, as well as implications for future teaching.

▶ **How will this approach to assessment fit with the requirements of Baseline Assessment?**

At present (2000), Baseline Assessment remains a statutory requirement for children as they enter the reception class, and takes place within the first seven weeks of each child's time in reception. It therefore takes place in the middle of the Foundation Stage but at the beginning of a child's time in the more formal setting of mainstream schooling. This system will not be reviewed until September 2002.

Currently there are many different systems used for Baseline Assessment, but usually where a child has been in a nursery setting prior to reception class and a record has been passed on to the reception teacher or school concerned, the Baseline Assessment will take account of what this shows.

Where a child moves from the nursery to reception class in the same school, this transition can be helped significantly by continuing to use the system recommended here in both nursery and reception. In many schools nursery staff are enlisted to help the reception teachers with the Baseline Assessment process. In any situation, passing on a record of achievement based on tracking significant achievement provides an excellent basis for planning, continuity and progression for reception teachers to build on.

However, regardless of what system for Baseline Assessment is used, nursery education staff are required to keep records of children's learning. A system such as the one recommended in this book fulfils the QCA requirements as already outlined and is easy to manage.

▶ **Should I involve the other staff I work with in recording children's achievements when assessment is the teacher's responsibility?**

It is true that assessment of the children is one of the responsibilities that the teacher in a school has towards the children in her/his class, but this does not mean that the work is not shared with other staff. In fact, other staff who are working with the children are just as likely to see significant achievement as the teacher, so a lot will be missed if other staff are *not* involved.

These days, in both nursery and reception classes, teachers should be part of a team of professionals who work with the children in the class. In reception it may be a trained nursery nurse, although more commonly it is a primary helper or classroom assistant. It may be that some support staff are not confident to write records at first and they will therefore need instead to talk to you about the achievements they have noticed. Time will need to be arranged for feedback sessions together to allow this to happen. Because of the differences in working hours between support staff and teachers, this may need to be discussed at school management level to ensure time is set aside to facilitate the involvement of all staff in assessment procedures.

The nursery team in a school usually consists of a trained nursery nurse with a child-care qualification working alongside the teacher. Child-care training normally involves carrying out many careful observations of children. Nursery teachers usually acknowledge that when it comes to carrying out detailed observations of children, nursery nurses are much better at it than teachers!

The difference between a 'significant achievement' approach to assessment and carrying out regular, detailed observations of each child is that staff are looking for significant *developments* rather than recording as much as possible of what a child does in a period of time. However, both approaches begin by sharing some necessary skills – for example, the ability to observe and to decide on the significance of what has been seen.

In order to involve support staff fully in the assessment process, sharing the advice in this book on how to find significant achievement will be an important exercise, either through early years staff meetings or through inservice training sessions which involve support staff.

It is worth noting that in local authority, private or voluntary day care, nursery or playgroup settings, it is *any* staff – regardless of qualifications – who are responsible for assessment of the children.

▶ How can I use records of significant achievement for planning when I am required by the school to write plans for the whole class every half-term?

Making long- and medium-term plans for the whole class is an important part of the planning process and helps to clarify the purpose of your teaching. The QCA *Curriculum Guidance for the Foundation Stage* (2000) is an aid to planning which takes a broad outlook on the curriculum, and writing your own plans based on this broad framework is essential. Your termly or half-termly plans will include the learning possibilities within areas of provision along with your broad learning intentions for some of the teacher-led activities you intend to provide. These kind of plans will highlight learning for groups of children and the whole class, not specific individuals.

Your records of significant achievement need to feed into your short-term (usually weekly) plans initially, reminding you of specific support and teaching that an individual will need within an activity or area of provision made for the class or groups of children. This may be things as widely different as supporting one child's pen control, setting up situations supporting one child to work collaboratively with another, or encouraging a child to dictate a story to you. Some of these specific plans may require more long-term strategies for groups of children, and future, mid- or long-term plans will need to take account of these.

In my book on early years planning and assessment *Right from the Start* (Hutchin, 1999), there is detailed and specific advice on planning and assessment in the early years and practical ways to link the two effectively.

▶ How do I record coverage and achievement across the whole early years curriculum?

The Tracking Significant Achievement system records children's achievements; using the matrix will keep track of what achievements have been recorded in different aspects of learning across the curriculum range, in both teacher-led and child-initiated activities.

Your written plans will record what you intended to teach and the experiences you provided for the children. Your assessment matrix will show you examples of the outcomes of your teaching and children's learning. However, a quick note or evaluation should be added on to your daily planning format, evaluating what you had planned by noting which children may need more of a particular experience, or an extension to it. This will then feed into the next set of plans.

▶ I believe assessing the development of the whole child is important, but how can I do it?

The way we have examined significant achievement in this book in fact contributes a great deal to looking at children's development in a holistic way. Highlighting the five aspects (social, physical, process, attitudes and concepts) within any particular achievement in any area of learning ensures that a broad view of learning is taken. Teachers beginning to base their assessments on observations of children at play, as recommended here, are always surprised by how much significant development and learning can be noted in many different areas and aspects of learning from one short observation of a child.

Although the approach outlined here looks for different aspects within an achievement such as social or physical skills, these are seen as separate areas of learning in the Early Learning Goals. This helps to ensure that a *comprehensive* holistic view of learning is taken, with some achievements highlighted separately as personal and social or physical development (e.g. settling in and independence or gross motor skills) whilst others may be recorded as an aspect of another achievement.

As stated in Chapter 2, children's learning is holistic – they do not learn in boxes under subject headings and records of genuinely significant achievements may be sometimes obviously attributable to one area of learning and at other times much more cross-curricular. The main thing is keeping records of significant development as they happen and using the matrix to ensure that a holistic view of each child is recorded.

Decisions about which areas of learning to keep records on will be partly up to you and your school. Although the most important areas for recording are language and literacy development, maths, and personal, social and emotional development, many feel that every curriculum area needs to be covered.

A holistic view of learning is aided in the early years by the way the six areas of learning have been developed. For example, scientific exploration and technology are seen as part of the all-inclusive heading *Knowledge and Understanding of the World*, along with ICT, history and geography.

▶ What should I do about a child who is not showing any significant achievement?

This shows that you have a good monitoring system and your matrix is working for you. First of all, perhaps it is just that you have not noticed what the child is doing. Teachers told us that, as they began to use this system, at first they only noticed very obvious significant achievement, then the brighter and the less able children. They felt that those in the middle ability range are always the most difficult to track. Some children are always more obvious than others and some, often quiet, children seem almost invisible. It could also be that you are looking for something *too* spectacular. Significant achievement is *anything* which you think would be important to write down about a child.

For the children you are finding difficulties in noticing significant achievement, you will need to plan to watch more closely. Track the child through a day or across a week. What does the child do? Is the child involved in discussion or activities? Who does the child play with? Where does the child position him/herself? Who does she/he talk to? Is the child in fact taking very small steps forward? Involve yourself in the child's play and activities; if she/he seems particularly shy and quiet at first, involve yourself alongside them until they are more used to your presence. All this might suggest areas of special interest or confidence that you can build on.

Asking the child about his/her likes and dislikes and things to do with home and family can often 'break the ice'. This may give you clues about what is going on. Involve other colleagues and support staff who work with the child, and talk with parents. Sometimes this investigation will provide an answer. It may be that there is a need for support or an extra challenge in a particular area. You may find there is a need to monitor the behaviour of some other children who may be excluding or upsetting the child in some way. In the reception class, there may be a need to rearrange class groupings or to tackle problems in the playground.

Once you begin to look in this way, you will either find that the achievements *have* been happening and you have missed them, or that your new understanding of the child will help you to plan so that they are more fully involved in classroom life and you involve yourself with them more – then achievements will start to show. *All* children should be showing significant achievement, regardless of their abilities. It is simply a matter of redefining significance for that child. Very tiny steps for one child are just as significant as more obvious leaps for another.

From time to time teachers have problems in noticing significant achievements for brighter children, and sometimes in nursery settings this may be a problem with the oldest group of children. The question to ask then is: *Are the learning experiences provided challenging enough for all the children?* A child who begins in the nursery or reception class already able to read, and whose mathematical ability is far in advance of the other children, will need to be provided with appropriate challenges. You may need to look more carefully at providing for other skills as well, such as social skills, which may be less well developed. Older children in the nursery may be spending a great deal of their time seemingly fully occupied, but if it is difficult to see any significant achievements, they will need greater challenges set for them, such as involving them in a longer-term project or investigation.

In *Right from the Start* (Hutchin, 1999) there is also a full discussion on this issue, but the main points can be summarised in the following way, showing what teachers can do about children they find it difficult to record achievements for. You may need to:

◆ build a closer relationship with the child;
◆ get more involved in her/his play and activities;
◆ do some observations;

◆ provide learning experiences to extend the child's own interests;

◆ set greater challenges for the child.

▶ How many times do you have to see significant achievement to write it down?

Recording significant achievement has a *formative* purpose – aiming to highlight the next step that a child needs. It therefore aids teaching. The important point in this question is how significance is defined. It may be very important to record the first time a child has done something new, such as mixing in with a group activity, or retelling a familiar story. Highlighting the circumstances which made it happen, including, where possible, the child's view of this, helps the teacher to allow it to happen again. For a different situation with another child, you may want to make just a mental note to yourself at this stage then see if it happens again in other circumstances.

▶ How do I get time to talk to all the children about their achievements and my learning intentions for them?

This question is addressed more fully in Chapter 6, but some brief answers here may be useful. In both teacher-led and child-initiated activities, participant observation is a key to teaching in the early years. All staff spend a lot of their time talking to individual children in the classroom and outside area. These are natural times for an assessment dialogue to take place. It is not difficult to talk to children about their achievements if you are there when they happen, have just observed them, or the child brings something to show you . You may need to change the emphasis in the things you say, to ensure they realise you think it is an achievement, and ask the child for her/his views too. Pride in achievements is more likely to grow from a conversation about the achievement where you specify what you think the achievement is, than from just praise on its own. Even if the child does not have much to tell you at first, once you have introduced the subject, the child will know what you feel is important and that you are interested in her/his opinion.

The important point is that this is not seen as an add-on extra, but part of your normal discussions with the children.

Of course, whilst working with one group you are bound to miss things that other children are doing – you will not be able to see everything. But if something really is significant, it is likely to happen again. Involving support staff in looking for significant achievement and talking with the children about their achievements will undoubtedly help. Keeping careful track of which children you have recorded achievements for will show you which children you need to plan to spend time with.

Talking to children about your learning intentions for them in the context of talking about their achievements means you are more likely to create the right learning intention. They are more likely to understand your intentions and to make them their own too.

▶ I do not always get a response when I ask some children about their achievements. Does this matter?

With very young children, new to school and institutional life, it is not surprising if we receive little response at first. They may not ever have been asked to reflect on something they have just done, even less a process skill you have noted, or a social achievement. Other children, however, may respond at length from the outset. Remember that the way in which you ask the question may be a significant factor in the type of response which results. It will be important to ask open-ended questions which invite the child to make more than a one-word answer. Some examples of these kind of questions are given in Chapter 2. The timing and the situation in which you ask the question may also influence how children respond. If they are busily engaged in another activity, or still involved in pursuing the same train of thought which you have highlighted as significant, it may be difficult for them to respond to your questions. Chapter 6 includes some more suggestions for how to introduce discussions on achievements.

For the children who do not respond to invitations to talk about their achievements, continue to ask and to talk about these, when the appropriate time arises. At first you may be answering your own questions, but at least you have invited the child to reflect. Just because you do not receive a response does not mean that what you have highlighted is not significant for the child. You may, however, wish to observe further to check more thoroughly what the significance was and to think of other ways of approaching the discussion.

▶ How can I support and assess bilingual pupils?

Many of the suggestions in Chapter 2 for creating a climate for learning provide the vital support that bilingual pupils will need. Several of the examples of children's learning used throughout the book are of bilingual children, including two of the children whose development is charted in Chapter 4. These should help to give some indications about both support and assessment.

However, it is worth drawing some of the points made together here. First and foremost, it is important that bilingual children feel that their language and culture are valued in school:

◆ Is it obvious to the children that their first languages are welcomed and seen as a positive asset in broadening the awareness of all the children in the class?
◆ Is there scope for bilingual pupils to use their first language?
◆ Can the children's first languages be heard in the classroom? This could be through the use of tapes, if there are no other speakers of the language in the class. Are these languages visible in some of the displays?

In planning and organising activities it will be helpful to consider the following:

◆ Do the children feel at ease to talk in their first language, even if you do not understand it ? They can be encouraged to use gesture and visual clues to help you understand.
◆ Does the activity build on existing knowledge and understanding?
◆ How can the activity be introduced so that it is accessible to all? Consider the possibility of using pictures, photos and other visual clues to demonstrate ideas and accompany the words you use. Story tapes and displays can also help.
◆ Which key words would it be useful to translate – for use,

for example, in turn-taking games or in helping children to understand routines?

◆ Make sure that you identify, use and reinforce the same words in English each time, so that the children can follow the strands in your talking .

◆ Make sure the child feels part of the group and that other children are supportive to them – you will need to explain to the other children that they speak another language and are learning to speak English and that they need help.

◆ In your planning, think about how an activity can extend the child's linguistic ability.

Considering these issues in relation to bilingual pupils is likely also to be a helpful approach for many other children who need support in their linguistic development.

▶ I do not find it easy to spot examples of concept development. What should I do?

First, the development of concepts takes time and very rarely happens as the result of one experience – there are many stages on the way. In the early stages of developing concepts children might just be making connections between one event and another, and only gradually will they be able to generalise over a range of situations. Becoming sensitive to these early developments takes time and practice, and it may be useful to record some of these. Your observations of children will help you to become aware of their levels of understanding; talking with the child will also give important clues to their thinking. It is often easier to note children's process skills than their understanding of a concept, but evaluating what their process skills show will help you spot the concept development.

▶ As I have not collected examples of significant achievement specifically related to Early Learning Goals, what should I be passing on to the child's next teacher?

As suggested in Chapter 1, the records to pass on should be the most recent examples of achievement for the child in various areas of learning. The Early Learning Goals relate to children at the *end* of the reception year and you will have been planning to cover the full curriculum, progressively leading towards these goals.

What you have collected will be very relevant to these, as they are specific to the child and demonstrate her/his current level of development. Even if the children from your class are going to different schools, some of which will not be using the same system of assessment, what you have recorded still provides very useful information about the child and the kind of experiences the next teacher should be providing. Your records will not be 'standardised', because they are formative, and reflect each child as an individual, but this is what makes them useful and relevant to the child and teacher.

Many schools also ask teachers to complete a summary statement for each area of learning, especially where children are moving on to new schools. The latest examples of achievements would be passed on with these short summaries.

▶ What should be shared with parents?

It is not just a question of *what* to show parents, but also *how* to get them involved. Some useful ways of involving parents are addressed in Chapter 6. It is important to tell parents from the outset, when the child first joins your class, about your record-keeping and assessment and invite them to contribute what is going on at home. Most parents welcome any opportunity to talk about their child's progress and to contribute their observations and knowledge of their own child, as well as their hopes and expectations. Their contributions will be vital to gaining a holistic view of the child.

6 Getting Started

So far in this book, we have examined what significant achievement can look like in early years classrooms, how to track it in individual children and how to develop this into a comprehensive assessment system for all children in this phase of education. The conditions teachers need to create in order to promote significant achievement have been outlined, as well as the teacher's role in organising both child-initiated and teacher-initiated activities: significant achievement should be happening in both of these kinds of activities. We have also stressed throughout that significant achievement does not just refer to tangible products that children produce, but to *all* achievement in the processes of learning - social and physical development and the development of attitudes, as well as process skills and concepts.

Tracking significant achievement requires teachers to:

◆ **observe** - *look for achievement*
◆ **involve the child** - *in talking about it and reflecting on it*
◆ **make the assessment** - *be clear about what is significant for the child*
◆ **record** - *write it down in the format suggested*
◆ **plan** - *what the child needs next*

The matrix suggested in Chapter 1 helps to keep track of what has been recorded for every child in the class and highlights any gaps.

The next questions are:

Where do we begin?

 and

How do we go about it?

Introducing anything new needs to be thought through and planned. It is important that this is done slowly and carefully, with time built in to review how it is going, or staff may feel overwhelmed and unable to create a manageable system which suits their needs. The first piece of advice, therefore, is: don't rush into it, take it a step at a time.

Over the past few years many LEAs have produced guidelines for early years assessment based on observing children. The practical advice on how to get started given here is based on the experience of teachers who have been involved in courses on significant achievement and the experiences of teachers who have introduced similar systems.

Getting started: some general principles

The following general principles are useful in planning the introduction of any new development or change, such as a new assessment system.

Build on what you are already doing

This approach to tracking significant achievement is by no means a new approach in early years teaching. In fact, it fits very well with the principles of good early years practice which have been advocated for many years, as well as with new developments.

For many teachers and nursery nurses, this approach builds on the observations they are making regularly on children and turns it into a *systematic* approach. What is most likely to be new is the inclusion of the child's *own* view of their achievement. For nursery staff, in particular, clarifying learning intentions throughout the provision made may also be something which is not done systematically. Both of these elements, however, build on previous approaches.

◆ The tradition of **observing** children and using observations for assessment of learning in early years education can be dated back to Susan Isaacs in the 1920s. Tracking significant achievement fits well with this.
◆ A more **systematic** and consistent approach to **planning** has been advocated, particularly from the 1980s onwards, in the early years as well as throughout education. In

particular, the link between planning and assessment of individual children has been widely stressed (e.g. Lally, 1991; Blenkin and Kelly, 1992).

◆ Involving **the child** in assessment has been tried and tested for several years in primary and early years education, particularly by teachers using the *Primary Language Record* (CLPE, 1988). With regard specifically to early years, some LEAs have incorporated this idea into their early years record-keeping system, although in a more generalised way than we are suggesting here.

◆ Involving **parents** in the assessment process, as well as sharing the records with them regularly, has also formed an important element in many of the early years assessment and record-keeping systems developed over recent years.

◆ Records of Achievement and **pupil profiles** have now been adopted throughout education.

◆ The **aspects of learning** highlighted in this approach have always been considered by early years staff to be of utmost importance and have formed the basis of much early years record-keeping in the past. *Patterns of Learning* (CLPE, 1990) also highlighted these aspects of learning and emphasised the development of reflectiveness. What may be new for some teachers is highlighting these aspects of learning within individual examples of achievement - for instance, the social aspects of a child's significant achievement in maths.

There may be many things in your current practice that you can build on. It is therefore important as a starting point to review and clarify what you are already doing, and consider how you can extend or modify this.

Start small

Introducing anything new which is very different from what you are currently doing needs to be gradual - trying to introduce a whole new system all at once is not likely to succeed without difficulties.

1 It is best to begin tracking significant achievement with just a few children - say three or four - for the first few weeks. You can then iron out some of the problems at the beginning and be learning how to do it most effectively at this stage. You will also be able to see in which areas of learning you find it easiest to spot and record significant achievement, and which elements of the system (e.g. involving the child, looking at process skills or concept development) you find most challenging.

2   In order to find out what is significant for the children in your pilot group, you may need to begin by watching them a little more closely. Participant observation (observing whilst you are involved with the child either in teacher- or child-initiated activities) will be the best way to do this. It will mean you can talk to the child about what they are doing as they are doing it, but make sure you are aware of what is really going on, by listening and watching, before you join in.

3   After the initial pilot study, some teachers in nursery and reception classes, where a group of children begin school every term, have tried starting the new system of assessment with just one term's new intake. Each term the new intake is added, making the introduction of the new system quite manageable. In the nursery school where I taught most recently, our new system was introduced in this way. Although it took five terms before *every* child's record was based on the new system, it certainly meant that it was manageable and we learnt how best to do it as we went along.

Start from what you do best

If until now you have concentrated on keeping records on some areas of the curriculum and not others (e.g. physical development, language development, maths), then you will probably find it easiest to spot significant achievement and to talk with the child about their learning in these areas. Start with these and then begin to include other areas.

Use the matrix from the beginning

However small your pilot group is, make sure you use the matrix from the beginning. In this way you will be able to see at a glance which areas of the curriculum you find easiest to spot significant achievement in and whether you are collecting examples of achievement for some children and not others.

Make time for regular review

As you are introducing the new system, make sure you build in times to review how it is going with other staff involved. As well as being able to resolve any difficulties as you go along, this will give you a clear sense of progress.

What follows are some practical examples of the strategies which teachers have tried and found successful in getting started.

Getting started with your class

PLANNING - Focusing more explicitly on learning possibilities and intentions

1   Review your planning, to make sure it incorporates areas of provision (e.g. construction, home corner, etc) as well as specific teacher-led activities. This means reviewing the learning possibilities within these areas of provision, looking at how these are resourced, how they cover the areas of learning, and planning how staff are to be involved.

2   Involve children in this planning and review of areas. Not only will this give them a clearer idea of the ways in which they can use the area, but it will also help them to articulate their own ideas and give you an insight into how children view what is on offer to them.

3   In your planning of teacher-initiated activities, make sure you clarify learning intentions - your reasons for introducing the activity and what you expect the children will learn. Sometimes your learning intentions may be quite specific to individual children but appropriate to many others in the group too. For older children, the teacher is more likely to be able to set a group learning intention.

SPOTTING significant achievement

1   As you work with the children or join in with their self-chosen activities, be observant of what they are *actually* doing, rather than what you *hope* they are doing. Build in time to participate with the children in any area of provision, listening and watching, as well as talking to

them. This will make it easier to see the achievements happening.

2 Make sure the children can find the resources they need, as well as being trained to put them away when they have finished with them. This will free staff from some of the menial management tasks which can take up a lot of valuable time.

3 Having a notepad available, to write down the achievement as it happens and whilst you are still with the child, will save time. This will be particularly useful with achievements which are not related to specific pieces of work, or products. The assessment and record is then made at the time it happened, rather than after school. Trying to remember after the event something that has occurred, or a comment that was made by a child in a busy classroom, is usually doomed to failure if it is not written down immediately.

TALKING with children about significant achievement

1 When significant achievement has occurred, talk to the child about it. This shows that you think it is important. It may be that the child does not reply or join in the conversation at this stage, because for some children this can take a long time. However, you will have made it clear to them that you have noticed and appreciate what they have achieved. Writing down whatever they have said about the achievement will also begin to give them an idea that you think their view is important.

2 You will need to clarify for every child what you think the specific achievement was, if necessary providing visual clues to help the child understand. This is, of course, easier with a product than a process or skill, but you can always take the child to the place where it occurred (e.g. the home corner), and say simply what you saw, along with giving some specific praise or feedback, and then ask the child about it. This will be particularly helpful for bilingual children new to English, even if the question you ask is a closed one at present - such as *'Did you like doing that?'* Later on, the questions can become more open-ended.

3   Make a time for small groups to share things they are proud of with other children, and include in this *process* rather than just *product* achievements - holding a pen, length of time doing something, etc.

4   Make a time to look through the children's records with them, showing them what you have collected and reading some of these out to them. This is one of the best ways to help them to become self-reflective and give them a clear idea of your learning intentions for them.

SHARING records with parents

1   Inform parents from the beginning of their child's time in school about your method of assessment and record-keeping. Make a time to talk to each parent about their child as she/he starts school, or before (on a home visit, or when the child comes to visit before commencing school). The points parents make about their child can be recorded - many schools ask parents to write something, or you can take notes of what the parent tells you. This can then be put in the child's record as a starting point for looking for achievements at school.

2   Share the whole record of achievement with the child's parents at parents' evenings. This will also be a good time to ask parents what the child is doing at home, and notes can be added to the record.

3   Parents of reception and nursery class children usually have a great deal of informal contact with their child's teacher: use this time to update them about significant achievement at school. They can also be asked regularly to give their views of the significant achievements they feel are taking place at home. Notes of these, with any relevant products (drawings, writing, etc), can be added to the record. This will also have a knock-on effect to the child's confidence in themselves and awareness of their own achievements. For working parents, photocopies of the recorded significant achievements can be made on the day they happen and the child can take them home. These can be used to keep the dialogue on what the child is achieving open with parents who do not have frequent contact with the school. Explain to them before their child starts that this is what you will be doing, and that you would also like them to send in notes

about any significant achievements they have noticed at home.

EXTENDING 'quality' time with the children

Of course, we all want as much quality time with children as possible, but there will always be some interruptions which are unavoidable. Making sure children can help themselves to resources, and are trained to tidy up after themselves, will allow staff more time without interruptions. It is surprising how often teachers forget the basic essentials in helping children to be independent in tidying up - for example, do you have a dustpan and brush beside the sand tray, a bin by the workshop table and writing area, well organised tools with clearly marked places to keep them, and clearly labelled storage trays?

TRACKING significant achievement

1   From the beginning, maintain a matrix including all the areas of learning you want to keep records on. Every time you have recorded an achievement, mark it off on the matrix (see Chapter 1).

2   Keep a regular check on the matrix to highlight which children you are finding it difficult to record; keep a check on whether you are recording the *breadth* of the aspects of learning (social, physical, concepts, etc) for each child.

3   Use the matrix to inform your planning, both short term (e.g. for specific children) and longer term (e.g. to improve your coverage of an area of learning).

Getting started with the school

INSET

Organising an INSET day for the whole school on assessment can be a very helpful starting point. In some primary school situations this may mean an INSET day specific to all staff in nursery and reception only. Staff involved could be encouraged to bring along some samples of children's work (including observations of processes of learning) to share and discuss together their significance for the children concerned.

Introduce the idea at a staff meeting

Introduce this approach to assessment at a staff meeting, using the framework suggested in Chapter 1. As for an INSET day, bringing along practical examples of significant achievement and the children's comments will be a useful starting point. Other staff can then be encouraged to look for examples in their own classes to bring to a future meeting.

Start with an interested colleague

The best approach may be to pair up with another member of staff who is also interested. It will be important to share with other team members in the nursery and reception from the beginning, so that they can be looking for significant achievement too.

Review current practice

At a whole-school level, reviewing the current practice for planning, assessment and record-keeping in every class will give a clear picture of what is happening now. This will then help you decide where and how to start.

Start small in each class, then review after half a term

The same approach should be used if several classes are starting at one time as if an individual class is starting: a pilot group, then review, followed by a gradual introduction to using for whole class.

Discuss what should be passed on to next teacher

In a primary school it is important that teachers from different year groups meet up to discuss *which* information is most useful to pass on. This could be done by discussing examples from children's records of achievement.

In nursery schools, it will be important to ask the reception teachers in the children's new schools for feedback on the records you pass on. They may also be using a similar system, or, through your involvement, may become interested in your approach. Sometimes, inter-school meetings can be organised to discuss this kind of issue.

Bibliography

The following publications are referred to in the text and/or are recommended reading for all those working with young children:

Blenkin, G. M. and Kelly, A.V. (eds), *Early Childhood Education: A Developmental Curriculum*, Paul Chapman Publishing, 1988.

Blenkin, G. M. and Kelly, A.V. (eds), *Assessment in Early Childhood Education*, Paul Chapman Publishing, 1992.

Bruce, T., *Early Childhood Education*, Hodder and Stoughton, 1987.

Bruner, J., 'What is Representation?', in Roberts, M. and Tamburrini, J. (eds) *Child Development 0-5*, Holmes McDougall, 1981.

CLPE (Centre for Language in Primary Education), *The Primary Language Record, Handbook for Teachers*, published originally by ILEA, 1988.

CLPE, *Patterns of Learning, The Primary Language Record and the National Curriculum*, Centre for Language in Primary Education,1990.

Clarke, Shirley, *Targeting Assessment in the Primary Classroom: Strategies for Planning, Assessment, Pupil Feedback and Target Setting*, Hodder and Stoughton, 1998.

Donaldson, M., *Children's Minds*, Collins/Fontana, 1978.

Drummond, M. J. *Assessing Children's Learning*, David Fulton, 1993.

HMI, *Aspects of Primary Education: The Education of Children Under Five*, HMSO, 1989.

Hurst, V., *Planning for Early Learning*, Paul Chapman Publishing, 1991.

Hutchin, Vicky, *Right from the Start: Effective Planning and Assessment in the Early Years*, Hodder and Stoughton, 1999.

Lally, M., *The Nursery Teacher in Action*, Paul Chapman Publishing, 1991.

QCA, *Curriculum Guidance for the Foundation Stage*, 2000.

QCA, *Early Learning Goals*, 1999.

Vygotsky, L., *Thought and Language*, MIT Press, Cambridge, Massachusetts, 1962.

Vygotsky, L., *Mind in Society*, Harvard University Press, 1978.

Wells, G., *The Meaning Makers: Children Learning Language and Using Language to Learn*, Hodder and Stoughton, 1986.